Collection of the Philosophical Research Society

A TIBETAN MANDALA

THE MANDALA IS A MAGICAL SYMBOL OF THE UNIVERSE, WHICH IS REPRESENTED AS A WALLED CITY WITH FOUR GATES SURROUNDED BY EMBLEMS OF THE SKY AND THE CIRCLES OF THE HEAVENLY WORLDS. IN THE CENTER OF THE MANDALA IS A FORMATION OF LOTUS PETALS ADORNED WITH THE SACRED LETTERS WHICH SIGNIFY THE MODES OF CONSCIOUSNESS. MANDALAS ARE USED IN THE DISCIPLINES OF MEDITATION

Collection of the Philosophical Research Society

THE BUDDHA OF THE FIVE HUNDRED LOHANS

THE BUDDHA IS HERE REPRESENTED IN MEDITATION, HIS ROBES ADORNED WITH THE FIGURES OF HIS SAINTS, EACH OF WHICH IS AN INTELLECTUAL EXTENSION OF HIS OWN CONSCIOUSNESS. THE FIGURE OF BRONZE AND LACQUER WAS FORMERLY IN THE PRIVATE COLLECTION OF THE EMPRESS DOWAGER OF CHINA

SELF-UNFOLDMENT
By Disciplines Of Realization

By Manly P. Hall

Releasing and developing
the inward perceptions...
Practical instructions in
the philosophy of disciplined
thinking and feeling...

THE PHILOSOPHICAL RESEARCH SOCIETY, INC.
Los Angeles, California

ISBN NO. 0-89314-524-6
L.C. 83-15142

Seventh Printing, 1983

Library of Congress Cataloging in Publication Data

Hall, Manly Palmer, 1901—
Self-unfoldment by disciplines of realization.

Reprint. Originally published: Los Angeles, CA: Philosophical Research Society, 1977, c1970.
1. Occult sciences. I. Title.
BF1999.H3345 1983 291.4'48 83-15142
ISBN 0-89314-524-6

Published by
THE PHILOSOPHICAL RESEARCH SOCIETY, INC.
3910 Los Feliz Boulevard, Los Angeles, CA 90027

Printed in the U.S.A.

CONTENTS

I

II

III

IV

V

VI

VII

VIII

IX

X

XI

XII

I

THEORY OF DISCIPLINES

THIS book will have to use words in an attempt to reveal to you something that cannot be put into words. Consideration of metaphysical disciplines must begin with a definition of terms, for only after having established the meaning of certain words can we proceed safely with this extremely abstract study. But success in your study will require that you develop an intuitive grasp of metaphysical implications.

Meditation is an inward contemplation of divine realities. The subjects of meditation are the aspects of Truth. Truth may be cognized only when the student is in a tranquil state. There must be no tension or effort.

Realization is the simultaneous understanding and acceptance of the divinity and the divine purpose in all things. Even more, it is the acceptance of things as they *are,* and the *rightness* of things as they are.

Illumination is a state of conscious at-one-ment with the Universal Principle—man's participation in Truth. The methods by which illumination may be achieved are called disciplines.

Discipline is the specific directing and controlling of personal action. Discipline results in complete self-mastery.

All discipline must be effortless—yet actual. Spiritual development is not the result of a desperate effort to be good. It is rather an inward realization of right which transmutes the whole nature into the likeness of Truth.*

I

Growth is natural to man. No one thinks of a flower trying to bloom, or of a tree trying to grow. The blossoming of the flower is a manifestation of universal law flowing through the plant; it is the will of the Infinite made manifest in the finite. Illumination is the blossoming of the soul in man; it is just as natural, simple, and inevitable as the flowering of the rose. The wise man does not try to be wise; wisdom is as natural to him as folly is common to ordinary mortals. Man does not have to try to be himself.

Effort is evidence of inconsistency in the individual. Most religious organizations impose strict rules and regulations upon their members. These rules and regulations consist principally of "thou shalt nots," the purpose being to force man into a state of grace by inhibiting and limiting him. Any individual who tries to crush out with brute force of will the vices within himself, achieves only inhibition and neurosis.

When through realization we come to understand the divine energy that causes us to exist and grow, we cease to impede its natural flow in and through ourselves. When through realization we become aware of this divine virtue within ourselves, our inner nature is enlightened, with the result that our outer nature inevitably is transmuted.

---

* In Zen Buddhism the way of illumination is called the "gateless gate." The Taoists of China describe it as the "effortless effort."

II

Metaphysical disciplines should not be directed toward material ends. The true mystic does not meditate or concentrate in an effort to attract to himself the things of the material world; nor does he attempt to find in meditation an escape from the responsibilities or problems of his objective life. This does not mean, however, that metaphysical disciplines produce *no* physical result. When a man puts his inner life in order, through meditation and realization, the result is a happier and better physical existence.

If you can be taught the philosophical life, that is, the effortless way to grow, you will have been established in the foundations of wisdom. If this book can reveal in some way through the insufficient medium of words the wordless truth that being wise is the most simple and natural state of the evolved man, a great and permanent good will be yours.

The Chinese goddess, Kuan Yin, the "Lady of Mercy," is depicted robed in flowing garments which are, to the Buddhist mind, symbolical of the cosmic pattern of life. Existence is really a patterned flowing toward the real; a motion in space; a flowing of all life toward wisdom and truth.

Metaphysical disciplines are not to be regarded as competitive exercises in which one vies with another in the magnitude of his imaginings, or yearns toward some metaphysical aristocracy. All metaphysical exercises worthy of the name are an unfolding of self into the light of virtue, beauty, and wisdom.

The illustration for this lesson is taken from the Zen school of Chinese art. It is the "lone traveler," a solitary

(*Chinese painting showing a strong Zen influence. In the author's collection.*)

THE PILGRIM, STAFF IN HAND, STANDS ON THE BRINK OF THE SENSORY SPHERE.

HE FACES OUT TOWARD THE SHADOWY FORMS OF THE DISTANT MOUNTAINS, SYMBOLS OF THE GREAT SPIRITUAL TRUTHS WHICH ALWAYS LIE BEYOND. BETWEEN THE SEA, THE GULF OF MAYA

monk standing on the edge of a great cliff gazing out into the mist. Far beyond rise dimly the shadows of high mountains in ageless contrast to gnarled and broken trees in the foreground.

Much has been said of the loneliness of wisdom, and how the Truth seeker becomes a pilgrim wandering from star to star. To the ignorant, the wise man is lonely because he abides in distant heights of the mind. But the wise man himself does not feel lonely. Wisdom brings him nearer to life; closer to the heart of the world than the foolish man can ever be. Bookishness may lead to loneliness, and scholarship may end in a battle of beliefs, but the wise man gazing off into space sees not an emptiness, but a space full of life, truth, and law.

A metaphysical student who tries to be more than he is, can be very lonely. Only a part of him has gone forward. He has renounced old attachments, but he has not grown up to new ideals. He has renounced material things, but he has not outgrown them. He clings to a little of ignorance and strives for a little of Truth. Such a man is lonely and miserable. Space around him is still a void, for he has not realized the immanence of Truth.

III

In terms of realization, Truth is the cosmic *fact,* and that *fact* is the most beautiful, the most noble, the most gentle, the most wise, the most desirable of all things. This Truth is not merely a word that can be defined, but it is a sufficiency toward which man grows. It is the absolute law that abides in the farthermost and the innermost. It is all-sufficient to the wise man. Only the real can perceive or value the real.

The ancient masters have told us that illumination, the final reward of discipline, comes suddenly—when "no man knoweth." At the end of the path is that state "desired of all men." It is impossible to say when illumination will come to any individual. It may come tomorrow, or it may come after ten thousand lives; but discipline inevitably will bring closer this day of liberation. Metaphysics promises man freedom, security, and wisdom only when he has elevated his own nature to the appreciation and realization of the Divine Plan.

PERSONAL APPLICATION

YOUR desire is to develop a practical philosophy of life that will assist in the solution of your personal problems, equip you for greater usefulness to yourself and others. Your first need is for acquaintance with the general subject of spiritual development, and then an outline of a practical metaphysical program you can adapt to your own particular needs.

All humanity is subject to discipline in some form. In the material world discipline leads to skill and efficiency; lack of this discipline must result in diminished earning power. Elbert Hubbard once said that the average untrained working man earns a hundred dollars a day, but ninety-five dollars must be deducted to pay the salaries of those who do his thinking for him and correct his mistakes.

People go to school to learn trades because of the realization that skill is necessary to economic survival. It is just as necessary to develop skill in the metaphysical sciences. Religion, the most exact of the sciences, is not to be mastered merely through prayer and fasting. You do not become a good bookkeeper through hoping, nor do you become a great philosopher by mere desire. You must subject yourself to philosophic disciplines, and work toward proficiency in the sacred sciences.

An aspiring few envision a larger purpose behind the visible world and its activities. The reward for increased efforts is fuller realization of spiritual truths.

Peace and security are not to be found by merely informing the mind or increasing the intellect. Regardless of how deeply a man feels, or how broadly he studies and improves himself outwardly, he is not complete until he has perfected his inner disposition. Until spiritual consciousness has tinctured and brought to perfection all the efforts of the intellect, man is not secure and not sufficient.

Material education is directed toward increasing the skill of mind and hand. It may also give man a working knowledge in the arts, crafts, and sciences. But modern education does not give the student any knowledge of his own inner self. The spirit, the soul, and the metaphysical parts of man find no place in scholasticism. The result is evident. Material knowledge does not bestow happiness. It has not resulted in honesty. It has failed to inspire integrity. Only spiritual knowledge can complete education, by conferring security, moral courage, and spiritual enlightenment.

The end of metaphysical education is not memorizing facts in a textbook, but the expression through trained and developed faculties of the convictions of the inner spiritual life. All the great systems of metaphysical philosophy have included disciplines intended to release and perfect the higher ideals of the individual.

All things being equal, the individual with the best education will gain the most through metaphysical discipline. Metaphysics is not to be regarded as a substitute for education, but these disciplines mean the most to those already informed on a large variety of subjects. The man who thinks he can gain, say, a technical knowledge of Latin through meditation, will be very disappointed.

Metaphysical disciplines had their origin in the oldest of religious systems. Schools of metaphysical thought have flourished in India for thousands of years, and existed in most of the great nations of the ancient world. The difference between metaphysics and theology is principally in the matter of discipline. Julian, the Apostate, the wisest and the most virtuous of the Roman Emperors, declared that only the noblest and most learned men were worthy to participate in religion. Plato taught that purity and self-discipline were the first essentials of the philosophic life. After Nero murdered his mother he was afraid to enter the Temple of the Mysteries, although by right he was the high priest of Rome.

The old rules and disciplines which Plato, Pythagoras, and Aristotle obeyed, have not been lost. For centuries they have been ignored by Western thinkers who emphasized only the objective values of life. The Buddhist monks of China, Siam, and Burma, and the Brahman priests of India, still know and live the old disciplines. Strangely enough, these disciplines are really very simple. It is their application that is difficult.

The purpose of these secret teachings is to release into manifestation the spiritual values in man. The great initiates of the ancient world bear witness to the efficacy of the disciplines. But we no longer live in the time of Plato or Aristotle. The race is confronted with a new social experience. Economics and industrialism have arisen to plague the souls of men. The old exercises must be adapted to modern life if they really are to accomplish their original purpose. Many efforts have been made to adapt metaphysical exercises to the tempo of modern thinking. For the most part these adaptations have failed. The failure is usually due to over-optimism on the part of both teacher and pupil. Oriental teachers coming to this country usually assume that their students are already well-advanced; in reality the average student has accomplished practically nothing in himself. The problem has been to work out a program which can not cause difficulty, misunderstanding, or abuse. It is seriously believed that it is impossible for the student to get himself into difficulty through the study of this book, and genuine progress can be made toward a fuller understanding of the old Mystery teachings.

The practice of metaphysical discipline will not immunize any individual against the experiences that are necessary to him in life. Metaphysics has no power over the laws of reincarnation and karma, but helps the student to understand and appreciate these laws as they work out in his own life. The law of cause and effect is inviolate in nature. Metaphysics will give you the courage to start right causes in motion, and patience to work out the effects of causes already set in motion. Metaphysics will not remove obstacles, suffering, poverty, or debt, but it will give you the intelligence to face these assorted ills with a good hope, a high integrity, and a sound conviction. Metaphysics strengthens character, and thus it will help you directly to gain mastery over any group of circumstances—by facing them fairly, solving them honestly.

The law of karma, or cause and effect, applied to the actions of man is the *raison d'etre* of all metaphysical disciplines. The student earns a better fate through discipline; hence it is inevitable that he will enjoy a better destiny. All causes produce effects consistent with themselves. If the life is put in order through philosophy and realization, the result is not only greater security at the present time, but a better future in lives to come.

In ancient times those who desired to devote their lives to the sacred sciences traveled into distant countries to study with great and learned masters. Pythagoras received candidates behind a curtain, and it was only after years of discipleship that his pupils were permitted to behold his face. The Pythagorean disciplines are typical of the old methods of development. Candidates for admission to his school brought a report of their character and conduct from leading citizens in their communities. They had to have achieved a high proficiency in mathematics, astronomy, and music, or they were not eligible. Pythagoras determined by metaphysical means the disciplines necessary for each of his disciples. These disciplines were rigidly enforced for varying periods of time, the maximum being twenty years. Under the personal supervision of the master and his more advanced students, the beginner progressed safely, protected from all of the dangers which arise from an incorrect interpretation of metaphysical truths.

Nearly twenty-five centuries have passed since the burning of the Pythagorean Institute at Krotona. One by one the old Mystery Schools have disappeared. The Truth seeker of today may no longer beg admission at the temple gates. The disciple must discipline himself. Apollonius of Tyana, who lived centuries after the death of Pythagoras. imposed upon himself all of the Pythagorean disciplines, including the vow of five years of silence. He assumed these disciplines voluntarily because he knew that they were essential to his spiritual development. This must be the attitude of the modern student. Evolution has brought to the average man the power to analyze and estimate his own character. It is no longer necessary for the priestcraft to show him the forces of right and wrong. Each man is now his own high priest, his own initiator, the master of his own metaphysical life. Having realized this, your own integrity must strengthen you for the path of discipleship.

ADAPTATION

AMONG my friends is a charming gentleman of pure Anglo-Saxon ancestry. His forefathers probably died on the field of Hastings, but this man looks like and thinks like a Chinese. Today he is an elderly gentleman with slanting, Oriental eyes and a scraggly white mustache of Confucian cut. He has devoted his entire life to the study of Chinese, and frequently is called upon by Chinese scholars to interpret for them the intricacies of their own language. This learned and kindly man is a geographical misfit. From the viewpoint of reincarnation, this is probably his first embodiment in an Occidental form.

Biographers of Ralph Waldo Emerson have referred to him as the "New England Brahman." His library included most of the Eastern classics, and his whole approach to philosophy was Hindu. These are outstanding examples, but each one of us has come to this present life from some other national or racial background. If you will study the faces and temperaments of people around you, you will observe how the law of reincarnation has brought together the ends of the earth.

Because each one of us has a different spiritual background; because reincarnation has given each of us a different evolutionary experience; and because karma has confronted each of us with different forms of compensation, we must each study and learn and grow in a different way. Philosophy is largely a matter of interpretation, and interpretation depends upon viewpoint. That is why, when two people of different spiritual experiences attempt to interpret a certain metaphysical idea, each will arrive at a different conclusion.

Each student must interpret metaphysics according to his own character and his own needs. As St. Paul said, one man's meat is another man's poison. This individuality in all men requires that any specific method of metaphysical development must be carefully adapted to each student. It is impossible to make an adaptation without considerable personal study of the student himself, and his reaction to different forms of knowledge. That is why this book must avoid any form of metaphysical discipline which might lead to injury or disappointment.

There are two great divisions of metaphysics, Eastern and Western. The Western branch had its beginnings in Egypt and Chaldea. The Eastern branch had its origin in the pre-Vedic cults of Trans-Himalaya.

The Western school developed along objective lines and found its greatest exponent in Plato, the most perfect among Greek philosophers. The Eastern school, essentially subjective in its psychology, achieved its highest proficiency in the teachings of Gautama Buddha.

In its psychology of life the Western world essentially is objective. The Occidental believes what he sees. He values physical things and physical life, strives after position and power. Modern industrialism with its high measure of efficiency and its entire lack of idealism, is the inevitable product of an objective philosophy perpetuated by a comparatively unphilosophical people.

To the Hindu the invisible is real, and the visible is an illusion. The Oriental mind perceives clearly the hierarchies of celestial power. The goal of Eastern idealism is complete renunciation of all physical attachments and all physical possessions. The Eastern sage exists for the sole purpose of achieving detachment. He dreams of the day when he will have nothing, while the Occidental dreams of the day when he will have everything. In the East, wisdom is wealth; in the West, physical and visible accumulations are most desired.

We know that all extremes are imperfect, and that in moderation lies the greatest virtue. So the wise man of today is trying to blend Eastern and Western thought, and achieve a balance between attachment and detachment; between possession and renunciation.

In our modern educational system millions of young people are taught the same thing. Knowledge becomes for them a mimeographed education in which spiritual values are entirely ignored. The emphasis on sports and social events blinds them to the more serious values of study.

In the East the foundations for a metaphysical life are laid in childhood. The average Hindu boy of twelve knows more about religion than the average American clergyman of sixty. Mysticism is a birthright in the East. In the West it must be sedulously achieved, often at the expense of economic security. I have seen a Brahman mendicant sitting beside the burning ghats along the Ganges who could neither read nor write, but who could recite the entire Veda from memory. The recitation was exceedingly rapid, and yet it took about fourteen days, as the Veda is considerably longer than the Old Testament of the Bible.

You may ask: "Did this holy man understand what he was reciting?" For the most part, the answer is yes; for this beggar is to be numbered among four million Hindus who have renounced all worldly possessions, home, and security, to wander from one sacred shrine to another. In the East this is called the religious life. No one would recommend to a Western Truth seeker to follow such a course, but as a Hindu pundit once told me: *"A man who gives his all for what he believes, can give no more."*

We are fundamentally a materialistic people and few are the Occidentals who are not in some measure bound by material values, attachments, and ambitions. Metaphysics is to us an avocation, a hobby, a luxury, a passing experience.

We must accept the materiality of our race as part of the divine plan. Like the prodigal son, we must metaphorically go down into Egypt and herd swine. In the end we shall be richer for all the experiences that we shall have gained; we shall be wiser and nobler for our journey in the land of darkness and error. The reward for our experience is to be truly greater than the angels, in acquiring wisdom, courage, vision, and truth.

Because we are very different from Easterners, and because we are different from the ancients, we must adapt their mystical philosophies to present conditions. We must be practical idealists with a clear understanding of our own limitations. All men naturally desire to be wise, but individuals and races must approach the problem of wisdom in various ways according to their own understanding and their own experience.

Metaphysically speaking, our materiality results in a condition of isolation. As long as we deny the reality of the superphysical worlds, so long they will remain closed to us. As long as we live by a material standard in a divine world, we isolate ourselves from those innumerable divine energies which fill all being and sustain all life. To the Easterner, God is indwelling, the very heart and substance of all things. To the Westerner, God is very distant, something which must be approached with fear and trembling as we might enter into the presence of a great monarch, prostrating ourselves before the splendor of the divine presence. In the quest for Truth these differences must be taken into consideration and spiritual disciplines skillfully adapted to various needs.

The tempo of Western living has unfitted us for the peculiar sedentary, meditative life of the East. A great Indian saint once was asked to come to America and teach. He raised his hands in horror, explaining that the confusion of Western life would be fatal to his highly sensitive nervous system. In a way, this same confusion is exceedingly detrimental to any Western student who attempts the contemplative life. The vibrations of a large Occidental city are discordant and react violently on the sensitive centers of the soul ganglia or sympathetic nervous system.

The physical body of the Western person has increased its resistance to external impulses and developed a shock-resistant mechanism, and thus he is more blunt, more obvious, less imaginative than the Oriental. It is necessary to his survival that he live constantly in the evident; also that he build philosophies to justify this course of procedure, and that he depreciate any other system of living. It is all part of an escape mechanism. It is not surprising, therefore, that the more sensitive type of Westerner accepts gladly the fragments of Oriental philosophy that come to the West. Eastern mysticism appeals to the soul starved by Western materialism. Unfortunately, exploitation often follows.

Several sincere Eastern teachers have come to America in the last fifty years as missionaries of Eastern philosophies. They have attracted wide attention and their doctrines have found great favor. But these teachers discovered that for some inexplicable reason the most serious of their Western students suffered, sickened, and died. The difficulty was that the Oriental had overestimated the spiritual understanding of his Western pupils. He was interested in great systems of philosophy, but his pupils were interested in his *personality*. They believed in him, and not in what he said. They brought all of their spiritual blindness to bear on the subject, with tragic results.

Various forms of yoga, breathing exercises, and kundalini stimulation are among the dangerous teachings which have come from the East. These teachings are perfectly reasonable and normal to the East Indian who devotes his life to the purification of his body and the unfoldment of the spiritual perceptions, but as a plaything for Occidental people who hope that they can breathe themselves into a state of grace, such systems are entirely inappropriate. When the typical American business man takes up yoga he has neither the appreciation to understand it nor the integrity to apply it. For him it is a dangerous experiment fully as unfortunate as introducing high-pressure economics into India.

When a student of metaphysics attempts to develop his superphysical faculties without proper instruction, psychism is ever-present. Accounts of psychic phenomena excite the imagination of the uninformed. Ouija boards, visions, trances, table-tippings, and crystal-gazing possess an insidious fascination. Phenomena become the proof of spiritual power, which is reminiscent of one of the yesterday yogis who proved his cosmic consciousness by driving an automobile down a business street without any gasoline. This exploit won him a veneration that wisdom can never expect. It is most important that any student of metaphysics who expects to make any true progress in the development of his inner life should refrain from all forms of psychism, and avoid psychic phenomena.

The best schools in both the East and the West warn their disciples against psychism and mediumship. In India, psychic phenomena are practiced by members of the lower grades of Yoga; never by students of Raja Yoga. The problem of psychism has been in mind throughout the preparation of this book, influencing the selection of certain disciplines of a positive and non-psychic quality. The sensitiveness to superphysical forces that the student of mysticism develops must be under the control of his personal will at all times, and must. under no conditions lead into mediumistic vagaries.

FIRST REALIZATION

The Wisdom Religion teaches us that while in personality we are many, in principle we are one. There is one spirit in all men. Though innumerable artificial barriers made by man divide and isolate us, we are truly of one substance and one purpose.

We are more than similar; we are identical. We are manifestations of the One and we bear witness in our own parts to the One. This kinship of life; this identity of purpose and end, makes us truly universal.

As surely as all plants grow out of the same earth, so all lives come out of the one life. We are all plants with roots in space, nourished by one energy, and growing up to reveal one intelligence. To the degree that man can perceive this unity, to that degree he is wise. As long as he can think always of this impersonal unity, he can avoid division and discord.

An understanding of philosophy reawakens the spirit in man and restores to him the realization of the One. Our keynote from now on will be THE UNIVERSALIZATION OF THE INDIVIDUAL; that is, the development of universal values in each student.

Begin your philosophic life by gaining an imperturbable realization of the life and of the Law, upon which you will build your meditation. Attempt in your own daily life the chemistry of vision; bring the best and highest ideals of yourself to bear upon each situation that arises. Live up to the best that you know, and observe how quickly problems will disappear. Everything that is difficult becomes easy when it is done with Truth as the criterion of action.

If you gain only a little understanding of life upon which you may build a positive and helpful philosophy you will have accomplished much. You can not achieve perfection in a day or even in one lifetime. But if you work toward it you will come closer and closer to understanding. This realization is your first step. Ponder well upon it, for upon the rock foundation of individual integrity you will build the House of Universal Understanding.

TO ATTEMPT TO LIVE BEYOND WHAT WE KNOW IS DANGEROUS. NOT TO LIVE UP TO WHAT WE KNOW, IS EQUALLY PERILOUS.

II

INWARD PERCEPTION

THE principal sources of this book's metaphysical doctrines are Oriental, but they have been supplemented with certain teachings from the Pythagorean and Platonic schools to make certain the preservation of the Western viewpoint, and to keep the subject matter balanced and complemented. The three principal systems from which the Oriental material is derived are:

(1) *Taoism,* the deepest and most subjective of the Chinese metaphysical schools. Taoism was founded in the 6th Century before the Christian Era by the obscure philosopher Lao-tze. The teachings of Taoism base upon the realization and understanding of the word *Tao.* This word has several translations which include: the *Way,* the *Truth,* the *Means,* and the *End.* According to the Taoists, the word *Tao* may be studied forever and still it will remain only a word. But if the inner nature be illumined the word suddenly becomes the key to all knowledge, all mysteries, and all the aspects of Truth.

(2) *Lamaism,* the strange teachings of the Buddhist monks who live in the highlands of central Tibet. The order was founded by a Hindu monk, Padma Sambhava,

who journeyed from central India over the Himalaya passes, driving oxen loaded with books. The deepest metaphysics of Lamaism is found in the writing of the sage Milarepa, who revealed a profound and beautiful philosophy concerning the secrets of the transcendental nature.

(3) *Zen,* the most metaphysical and mystical sect of Buddhism. The word *zen* means realization, and the monks of this school are devoted to the inward perception of Buddhist Truth. The order of Zen was founded more than a thousand years ago by a Hindu Buddhist monk named Daruma, or Bodhidharma. The sect was founded in China and spread through Korea and Japan. Daruma was the thirty-third patriarch of Indian Buddhism.

I

In order that this instruction may succeed, it must be assumed that you are willing to begin with fundamentals. If you already have practiced occult exercises given out by schools, movements, or individuals, it is asked that you discontinue these during study of this book. It is impossible to successfully mix systems of metaphysical disciplines.

Such disciplines include any form of concentration, development exercises, breathing exercises, or special mental attitudes or affirmations for health, success, or any other material concern.

While you must clean your mental slate, it is not necessary that you discontinue the literature of, or your membership in, metaphysical organizations. But in your reading do not include books that are entirely inconsistent with the instruction in these pages. Every human being has the right to seek knowledge everywhere, and it is the purpose of this book to assist you to understand all of the great religions and philosophies of the world. There is no desire to place an unreasonable limitation upon your thought or action; but co-operation and sincere effort are asked for during the time in which you actually are studying these pages.

If you have been a student of the occult sciences for a number of years and have already received a groundwork from a reputable organization, the desire behind this book is that you may come to a fuller appreciation of the work that you have accomplished, thus to gain a new facility in applying principles to the problems of life.

As a student of metaphysics, you may expect very little encouragement from those about you; be prepared to resist the encroachment of circumstances. The true mystic is sustained by his own spiritual understanding. The source of all truth and inspiration is within. When you have developed this inner realization you will have gained a strength and peace which the material world can never take from you. Spiritual knowledge bestows security under any and all conditions.

The disciplines of meditation and realization require a new function of the consciousness. The mental processes must give place to an inward mystical perception that is not thinking, but knowing. The result is realization, an indefinable state of consciousness closely associated with what psychologists term the "mystical experience."

This supermental condition of awareness is described by the ancient philosophers as a "divine state." Proclus said that he was "lifted up into a participation with reality," that he "perceived all things clearly," and that he was "possessed by Truth."

Realization results from discipline. Discipline has long been interpreted as self-control, or as some would say, "the overcoming of the lower nature." The difficulty is that such words as "conquest" and "overcoming" suggest an entirely inconsistent aggressiveness of technique. The true metaphysician is not a wearied man wrestling with his lower nature; rather he is poised and relaxed, achieving through realization instead of conflict. Avoid the process of suffering your way into a spiritual state. A student who constantly must curb his animal nature by various types of vicarious flagellation will have to learn personal detachment.

Metaphysics acknowledges the fundamental that all human beings are imperfect. It demands effort, not perfection, at this stage of evolution.

In each human being there is a conflict between ideals and actions. We each know better than we do. The fact that we are not perfect should not lead to discouragement, but to a conscientious desire to improve by an intelligent process. Many people have ruined their lives by contemplating their mistakes and ignoring their opportunities. It is the goal of philosophy to order the lives of men. In a properly ordered existence the superior part in man controls and directs the inferior part; that is, the spirit controls the mind, and the mind controls the body.

Do not browbeat your faults. The moment the tension of effort arises, failure is inevitable. Those who try desperately to live up to certain moral virtues are constantly failing. All self-government arises from inner realization which automatically overcomes the resistance of the outer personality and accomplishes reform. In metaphysical disciplines you do not kill out faults; you change the focus of the mind.

That upon which we focus our attention is real, and that from which we remove our attention ceases to exist.

Do not try to destroy evil; posit good. Do not destroy the body; posit the consciousness. Do not attempt to destroy vices; posit virtues.

II

Metaphysics is based upon law. Law is the will of the universe for itself and its creations. Law is absolute and immutable.

Many metaphysicians have an erroneous concept of the meaning of Law. We hear about laws of abundance, laws of health, and others. Most of these people are invoking such laws for something they want. This concept is unreasonable and not to be entertained. The Law is the unchanging fact of existence; it is the Law that makes the practice of metaphysical disciplines possible. The Law serves no individual; all life serves Law.

The Law, according to the esotericists, is the inevitable, complete, and sufficient Truth by which all things were created, by which all things are sustained, and by which all things ultimately achieve their purposes. The Law is ever-flowing Reality, the ever-flowing Truth, the Rightness in everything which enfolds everything. If you walk down the street surrounded by a seething mass of humanity, all appears to be chaos; but to the inward perception it is evident that each human being in the mass is fulfilling his own destiny according to Law. Whatever we do is judged by Law. Wherever we go, we abide in the Law. To the metaphysician, Law is eternal right, absolute truth, and complete sufficiency.

According to the ancients, the Law is life; it is eternal self-living truth; it is the source and cause of all the countless forms of life, but it is itself universal and indivisible. Man's inward nature abides in and with the Law. It is only to the degree that his outward senses obscure this fact that his mind dwells in the sphere of uncertainty.

Of all the arts and sciences, living is the most important and the most exact. Living is a motion toward perfection through Law. The disciplines of meditation and realization enrich and perfect living by developing the understanding. By understanding we gain reason, and reason in turn bestows the courage and integrity necessary to high accomplishment.

III

Many modern schools place their disciplines on a time basis, but time has little place in the matter of growth. One may practice certain disciplines for ten years and still not be ready for any further enlightenment; or one may practice only a few weeks and be prepared for further instruction. The time that it requires to release the inner faculties depends upon the amount of spiritual enlightenment that has been brought forward from the previous life. It may be necessary to practice the disciplines for a number of years before the maximum results are achieved. If you are discouraged easily, or inconstant in your devotion to the subject, the benefits will be proportionately diminished.

These disciplines will not bring about miraculous changes overnight. But if they are applied conscientiously over a long period of time they will enrich the character and make you more capable of perceiving and understanding the mysteries of life.

KARMIC CULMINATION

IMPROVEMENT sets in motion the law of karma. To the degree that you improve, to that degree you will find increased opportunity.

One word of warning at this point is important. When you begin metaphysical exercises a certain definite change takes place within yourself. Feel confident that you are protected from any physiological disturbances; but nothing can protect you from the law of karma. This law has a way of speeding up, with the result that study of this kind will almost certainly increase your personal problems. You start paying karmic debts faster. This is important eventually, but is sometimes embarrassing at the moment.

You must be prepared to face certain disagreeable and difficult situations. They will show up the minute you begin to study. It is a process of purification in which the consciousness is throwing off certain negative parts of itself. When the body throws off poisons physically, we have sickness; when the soul starts throwing off poisons, we also have disturbances. These frequently take the form of difficulties with persons around us, financial problems, and temperamental difficulties. The thing to be remembered under such circumstances is that the paying of these debts by speeding up karma cleanses the subjective nature and prepares it to receive metaphysical instruction. Therefore do not be surprised if some of your difficulties multiply themselves.

It is encouraging to remember that the wisdom of nature never permits any individual to be confronted with insurmountable obstacles. Many fail in their problems, but this failure is not due to any lack of their possessing the potential power to succeed. Generally the problems which confront the metaphysician are adjusted to his increasing consciousness, and if he will live what he believes he will find the obstacles rather quickly dissipated, leaving behind only a wealth of experience and a deeper appreciation of values.

PREPARATION OF ENVIRONMENT

THERE are two kinds of environment, external and internal. External environment is made up of the outside world with its problems and attachments. Internal environment consists of the personality itself, which is a compound of impulses, desires, emotions, thoughts, and ideals. Man's physical life is an interplay of these internal and external factors, frequently in conflict and seldom brought under the discipline of the will.

It is obviously impossible for the average man to dominate his world. But he can master the impulses within himself, and by so doing achieve liberation from the pressure of external environment. Most great world philosophies teach that to conquer self is more than to conquer the world. Such a statement may seem platitudinous, but it is an important spiritual truth which will become more apparent to you as you proceed with your studies.

Man's internal environment is as yet imperfectly controlled by will and consciousness. It is, therefore, erratic and inconstant. The imperfections of this lower self impede the flow of energy from the spiritual nature. The purpose of self-discipline is to order and reform the lower self that it may no longer be an obstacle to the purpose of the spirit.

In the terms of Taoism, man stands in his own light—that is, between himself and that which he most desires.

What we are prevents us from being what we desire to be. Discipline applied to thought and action enables the student to get out of his own way.

Next to what we are, our great problem is what we have. Possessions result in possessiveness or fear. Both of these emotions cause worry. A worried man is full of his own problems, and there is little place in his nature for the contemplation of the divine realities. There is an instructive old Chinese picture of a man who has great wealth which he is carrying on his back in a huge sack. The bag is so large that he cannot see where he is going or where he has come from, and smugly contented with his possessions he is stepping off the edge of a cliff.

A rich man has external wealth of a fragile and impermanent nature. A proud or egotistic man has the internal equivalent of physical wealth. He is weighed down with the sense of his own importance. Anything that we have, even if it be only a high estimation of ourselves, is an impediment to progress. The greatest of all burdens is self-pride. A man can give away what he has, but only years of discipline can release him from the vanity of his own importance.

A wise man living in the physical world does not desire wealth. He desires peace and security, regarding contentment as more than riches. The sincere student, likewise, does not desire the gratification of his ego, but an internal well-being which is more than all the treasures of the earth. He does not desire to be greater than another man. He has come to the realization that greatness is relative and illusionary. The student, therefore, seeks first the Law and its workings, gaining therefrom the treasures of wisdom.

Do not feel discouraged if you encounter some small

difficulties in establishing the philosophic life within yourself. One of the great problems of Western living is interruption. The Truth seeker is constantly beset by interruptions that tend to divert him from his spiritual ideals. These unexpected happenings are a testing of his one-pointedness. They are external interruptions and will continue as long as man's internal life is negative to his external environment. However, when discipline makes the inner life positive and renders the environment negative, such interruptions cannot occur.

Tibetan monks are taught to meditate beside a great clanging bell. In time they reach a condition of detachment from the material life which enables them to be entirely oblivious of the sound. The distractions of life are appropriate parts of metaphysical training. They demand a concentration which greatly strengthens the will power of the student. For this reason it is inadvisable to hide in some secluded spot or retire from the world. Such a process negates the character and makes the student weaker when later confronted with stress.

Socrates was asked by a disciple where was the best place to begin the study of the sacred sciences. He answered instantly, "Where you are." Many Truth seekers constantly talk about their plans to "get away from it all" with the hope of roosting on the top of some distant peak where nothing is to be heard but the soft, timid voices of nature. As far as I have been able to observe, none of these sensitive folk ever accomplishes anything physically or metaphysically.

No doubt it is helpful on occasion to leave civilization for a short time to recuperate our forces, but if such a vacation becomes too extended character and integrity suffer. St. Simeon Stylites sat for forty years on the top of a column in the Libyan Desert, drawing up his food in a bucket. By this useless austerity he prevented himself from being of any use to anyone, including himself. We can understand easily why many people get tired of the stress of living, but no man ever achieved anything by running away. Western bodies are so built that it is perfectly possible to develop spiritually and at the same time fulfill our part in the social plan. To repeat the words of Socrates: *"The place to study is where you are."* Incidentally, *"now is the accepted time."* If you wait until you have time, you will never live to achieve the goal you seek.

Even if you remain in civilization it is quite possible to develop a wrong attitude which will destroy any good that experience might give you. There are many metaphysicians who can look a fact in the face and then deny it with a series of affirmations. Many of us have seen an individual sneezing violently whose philosophy of life taught that bodily ills were an illusion; but he had not learned not to sit in a draft. Also to be remembered is the elderly lady suffering from caffeine poisoning who persisted in trying to "deny" the caffeine right out of the several cups of coffee that she drank for breakfast every morning. There was also "God's perfect child" who had been brought up in an environment of platitudes, and yet was the pest of the neighborhood.

A philosophy of evasion is just as bad as running away yourself. There are many pseudo-metaphysicians who could live a thousand years without experiencing anything because their philosophy has taken away the privilege of experience. When metaphysics teaches you that divine law pervades all things, you must be extremely careful not to resolve this fact into a platitude. Do not start affirming that everything is all right when it evidently is not. Such a process is autohypnosis. When a small mind takes hold of a big idea, chaos is inevitable. Philosophy does not make wrong right, but it helps you to see the universal reality that circumscribes and orders all existence.

Realization must be built upon a sufficient knowledge. When knowledge is sufficient, there is no need for affirmations.

PURIFICATION

THE cleansing of the life through discipline is called purification. The early disciplines are properly described as "cathartic" because they really purge the life of negative or useless qualities. *The discipline must be effortless;* that is, with a gentle motion toward virtue by outgrowing useless attitudes and opinions which are detrimental to the harmony of life. The cathartic disciplines were advocated by the Platonic school as the most normal, most gentle, and most effective method of eliminating vices and faults.

Bodily purification is the first step. However, overemphasis on diet as a factor has frequently caused many difficulties. The body harmony usually is corrupted more by the thoughts and emotions than by food. Hence, while purity of body is necessary, we can not diet ourselves into a state of realization.

DIET

MODERATION is the greatest of the virtues and diet should be moderated to the peculiar needs of the individual. If you are now studying metaphysics for the first time, do not take an extreme attitude toward diet. If you have long studied the spiritual sciences you may already have developed a diet suitable to your own needs. A sudden fanatical change in any habit is very likely to cause unnecessary suffering; even tragedy. The metaphysician refines diet by eating less of very heavy foods, but he does not starve himself to death.

It is important also not to view a meal as a lapse into sin and apologize to yourself or others for the fact that you still need food. A meal to be useful to the body should be pleasant, tasteful, and enjoyable. It is not a disgrace to eat, but it is a disgrace to eat too much, unwisely, and uncomfortably.

The problem of vegetarianism is ever-present. If you are already a vegetarian and find that such a diet is suitable to you, the problem is well in hand. If you are not a vegetarian, do not stop meat eating at the beginning of your study, but rather eat somewhat more lightly of meat foods until you are satisfied that such a diet would be suitable. Theoretically vegetarianism is a great success, but my experience has shown conclusively that like nearly all virtues it can lead to serious trouble. This is particularly true for persons suffering from certain chronic diseases who would find their condition seriously impaired by any sudden change.

To vegetarians a special word of warning: Do not use starches as a substitute for meat or you will be worse off than you were before. A balanced vegetarian diet requires considerable time and thought. No one should try to live exclusively on raw fruit and vegetables unless he has personally experimented in this matter over a number of years. Remember that the East Indian mendicant does not have to contend with the strain and tension of Western living. Sitting quietly under a tree he performs no heavy exertion as he meditates the greater part of the time. A diet suitable for him is not suitable for you.

To quote Socrates again: "In all things, not too much." That means not too much food, and not too much enthusiasm in the matter of trying to get along without food. Fasting or extended periods of special eating should be undertaken only under the supervision of a trained and qualified dietitian. Experiments in starvation are usually unfortunate for amateurs.

EXERCISE

VIOLENT or unaccustomed exercise is a dangerous intemperance. It shortens life, exhausts energy resources and leaves the individual unfit for the responsibilities of daily living and thinking. It is not this book's purpose to discourage the man who wants to do his five minute setting-up exercise in the morning; the desire is only to remind the enthusiastic that physical exercise should be approached with moderation.

Exercise should be closely related to the daily life. It is very seldom necessary for a housewife to exercise. She walks many miles each day fulfilling her household duties. The Zen monks teach: No man should walk unless he is going somewhere. As your understanding of esoteric traditions increases you will realize that a moderate amount of exercise will come naturally; beyond this point it is unnecessary for you to go, unless you are confronted with some particular problem.

Students of philosophy can not be expected to excel in competitive athletics. Solon was asked to go to the games to see a great Greek athlete who could swim like a fish, jump like a deer, and run like a hare. He declined with thanks, declaring that it was not seemly that a human being should imitate animals. He added that if they could find a man who thought like the gods he would be glad to go.

Philosophers in their exercises seek to gain esthetic expression. They cultivate particularly the dance, which they regard as the perfect esthetic expression. It imparts something of the cosmic motion to the movements of the body, developing grace and rhythm.

FADS

THE philosopher is attempting to attain an eternal existence. He is striving for release from impermanent attitudes, beliefs, and habits. It is very necessary, therefore, that he achieve a detachment from all transitory matters such as politics, customs, and most of all, fads. This does not mean taking no interest in social progress, for all great philosophers have been sociologists. But he must stop fuming and fussing over this candidate and that party, and get to the place where he can perceive that all the varied and often contradictory procedures of mankind are contributing to an eternal pattern. Growth, integrity, and ultimate perfection are inevitable. There is nothing more disheartening to see than a group fretting itself into a frenzy determining whether a certain political party is going to overthrow civilization.

That which is real can never be destroyed, and that which is unreal can never be preserved. The wise man detaches himself from inconsequential controversies.

Fads are very much like politics. They arise in religion

periodically, and truly are the bane of philosophy. Just when a student gets nicely started in a system of discipline some brand-new notion comes along and off he goes on a tangent. Health fads are notorious—first it is walnuts, then Bulgarian bacillus, then orange juice. Metaphysical students who expect to get somewhere are uninfluenced by fads that have their roots in propaganda, and resist the temptation to try the so-called panaceas.

As in foods, so in clothing, and all the affairs of your life. Do not allow your attention to wander off into styles and fashions. Keeping detached from all such matters, live normally, eat normally, dress simply, and save your energy for the things in which you believe. You will save money and be far happier in the end.

ORGANIZATIONS

ORGANIZATIONS are a habit in religion. For centuries religious-minded people have belonged to something, and in consequence have decided that "belonging" is necessary. Metaphysical organizations have accumulated a rather unsavory reputation. Most of them are entirely static, and the few that remain dynamic are definitely reactionary.

The principal function of metaphysical organizations is to bolster up the mutual courage of the members. They do not give individual consideration; all members get the same teaching regardless of their fitness.

The wise person is not a "joiner." He is an individual thinking his own thoughts and building his own life through increase of knowledge and personal consecration.

It may be harder to accomplish by himself, but the results of personal accomplishment are the most satisfactory.

SECOND REALIZATION

Our second realization is derived from the teachings of Taoism regarding universal motion. According to the teachings of Lao-tze, all growth toward the real must be achieved through meditating upon the word TAO as interpreted in terms of rhythmic motion. Life must flow harmoniously from experience to experience, from incident to incident, and from condition to condition, without the consciousness of interruption.

The mind with its thoughts, the emotional nature with its feelings and impulses, and the physical body with its movements and patterns, must proceed harmoniously from one phase of activity to another. There must be no breaks in the patterns, no interruptions in the tempo or temper of living.

The contrast of viewpoints may be realized from a comparison of Oriental and Occidental music. To the Eastern ear, Western musical composition, because of the numerous breaks and changes in rhythm and accentuated pauses, is said to be full of holes, brief interludes of silence that cut in and break up the sound patterns. To Eastern ears these pauses and breaks are distinctly unpleasant. On the other hand, the old sacred music of Asia sounds monotonous to Western ears because it lacks these mathematically broken patterns.

Practice the realization of uninterrupted motion. Perceive the relationship between the incidents of daily action, and attempt to flow from one mode of experience to another without any appreciable interval of adjustment.

For example, if the telephone rings while you are engaged in the contemplation of some abstract truth do not permit this incident to be regarded, even for a moment, as an interruption. Include it in the meditation itself as a phase or part of soul-experience. Remember that all action is necessary, useful, expedient, or pleasant —is part of a definite order. If the incident be essentially of a disagreeable nature and the interruption is of an unpleasant kind, accept it as a phase of universal discipline. Refuse within yourself to be moved from your inward foundation of right. On the other hand, do not ignore the so-called interruption. Accept it. Perform the duties which it may entail, but include it within your realization of TAO. That is an ordered motion.

The keynote of your realization should be: FLOWING THROUGH LIFE WITH THE LAW. Do not permit yourself the extravagance of any useless expenditure of energy. Adjust to unexpected conditions. Let the expected and the unexpected be accepted with equal placidity.

III

COMMUNITIES

RELIGIOUS communities have failed consistently ever since a disgruntled disciple burned the Pythagorean institute at Crotona over the heads of Pythagoras and his followers. The Pythagorean community was the first religious community in history, and its fate has been reflected in the fate of all those that have followed it. It is very difficult for spiritual-minded people to live together. Community life introverts the thoughts of the members until their own particular organization becomes the axis of the universe. There is no question as to the sincerity of some religious communities, but there is a grave question as to the amount of actual good accomplished by them.

The existing social system is part of the plan for human perfection, in the general acknowledgment that infinite wisdom guides all natural activity. If that be true this heartless, material world is here for a reason. Those who segregate themselves and refuse to face the problems of social existence are simply trying to evade the Law. Such evasion being impossible, ultimately the evaders are thrown back again into society, weakened by years of isolation and rendered unfit for the duties of citizenship.

A retreat to which an individual may go at certain times, like the rest houses of India, has its uses in this troubled world, but to live for many years in a religious community weakens the individual for a return to active life among men. Prejudices result from an impractical attitude toward life. Determine not to run away to practice your virtues, but instead apply them *where you are* and under the conditions where they will accomplish the greatest good.

CONTINENCE

IN the early centuries of the Christian Church some of the fathers got together and decided that this material world belonged to Satan, and if they could depopulate the earth by preventing marriage the souls of men would thus escape from the grip of the Adversary. This idea failed because of the vast number of gentiles who refused to be converted. But this concept has not been allowed to die; it reappears under various metaphysical guises to complicate the issues of life.

On the subject of continence, various irrational attitudes have contributed greatly to the scientific disapproval of metaphysical teachings. Cults teaching a wide gamut of notions ranging from chastity to free love have seriously misrepresented a noble ideal. Most metaphysical organizations impose obligations upon their members with little regard for consequences. A fact which can be substantiated by physicians is that county hospitals and asylums all too often have the problem of trying to reclaim metaphysical wreckage traceable to unnatural modes of living.

It is not wise to take vows and oaths or make promises which involve unborn tomorrow. Nor should individuals obligate themselves to a method of living entirely beyond their comprehension, and too advanced for their physiological structure. It is to be stated firmly that growth is a gradual and natural unfoldment into Truth, and so it is unnecssary to impose any regulations upon the individual in metaphysical matters. The disciplines advocated in this book result in an emergence into virtue. There is no forcing, no struggling, no trying to be what you are not, but rather an awakening into values and realization.

There is no requirement that any student should suddenly change his entire method of living; in fact, such an action could only be detrimental. What is asked is that you refine and ennoble all of your relationships, and attempt to understand more perfectly the laws of life. If you will study the metaphysical doctrines set forth you will gain a realization which in time will lift you to a high standard of thinking and living.

Instead of limiting your external life, unfold your inner life. Your physical nature then will gradually refine itself, and you will find the qualities which you desire unfolding naturally within you.

BLACK MAGIC

CERTAIN central African witch doctors develop temporary clairvoyance by the use of intoxicating herbs. The sect of the Assassins in Irak uses hashish to dominate its members. It is written that even some of the heretical sects of Christianity produced a pseudoclairvoyance by drugging the communion cup. There are a number of ways of giving a false illumination to the unwary.

The Yogis of India, by mental exercises, create a self-hypnosis which enables them to permit themselves to be buried alive for a number of days and later be resuscitated. The natives of the Fiji Islands walk safely over beds of hot coals. Indian tribes of California still preserve a fire-eating ceremony. These apparently impossible feats are accomplished by the devotees first throwing their minds into a state of ecstasis. The practical value of these various demonstrations may be questioned, but the sincerity of those who practice them is unquestioned.

The Western occultist attempting to perfect his spiritual nature does not want to fall back into the negative practices of primitive sorcery. There is abundant proof of many primitive methods of working magic in all parts of the world, from the Haitian papaloys to the Islamic dervishes and fakirs.

There is a definite similarity between an evangelical revival and a congregation of the leopard men in the Belgian Congo. There is also something reminiscent of the miraculous mango tree in the modern habit of blessing empty pocketbooks and trying to produce something out of nothing. Metaphysics is intended to produce philosophers, not fakirs.

Many modern metaphysical organizations are practicing sorcery and do not know it. A sorcerer is a person who attempts by some special art to divert the forces of nature to his own personal ends. All forced growth is sorcery. Any individual trying to dominate his environment without rising above it is a sorcerer. People who attempt to use religious exercises for monetary gain, to lift mortgages, or get rid of undesired relatives, are sorcerers. The true purpose of metaphysics is to perfect the inner self in wisdom, virtue, and understanding, and any other use of metaphysical power is likely to result in black magic. The black magician may enjoy a temporary material success, but he is making a heavy karma that will have to be paid in future lives in terms of misery and suffering.

METHODS OF DEVELOPMENT

THERE are positive metaphysical exercises which purify the body, normalize function, and protect health. These exercises are devised to regulate circulation and nerve function, and result in greater relaxation and a greater attunement between all the parts of the physical fabric. The object of these exercises, however, is not the perfection of the body for its own end, but that the body may become a better instrument of enlightened purpose. Once the student can control his body he can control the innumerable emotions and impulses which arise in the body and interfere with the natural flow of consciousness.

The Eastern schools are extremely strict. They demand a complete control of the body, emotion, and thought. It is not unusual to find an Eastern holy man who can control the beating of his own heart or stop the circulation of the blood in any part of his body. At the same time the quality of harmlessness is posited in the mind, completely overcoming any destructive impulses or critical thoughts. It is well-attested that a holy man has been seen asleep in the jungle with the body of a lion for a pillow. It is widely believed throughout Asia that no animal, reptile, or insect will injure a holy man, because of the constructive vibrations which he has set up in his own nature.

The Eastern disciplines are intended to transfer the rulership of life from the animal soul to the divine con-

POSTURE IS ESTABLISHED IN THE LAW. THE STUDENT SEATS HIMSELF IN THE DISCIPLINES AND BECOMES IMMOVABLE. THE PHYSICAL PATTERNS ASSUMED DURING MEDITATION ARE SYMBOLIC OF THE RELATIONS WHICH ARE CAUSED TO EXIST BETWEEN THE DISCIPLE AND THE EXTERNAL WORLD

sciousness. Breathing exercises, postures, and various forms of discipline are aimed at the creation, in mind, emotions, and body, of channels for the release of inner integrity. As earlier mentioned, Eastern disciplines are not suited for Western minds or Western bodies, and their use is not advocated. The same ends are to be achieved by gentler and less strenuous ways. This has been proved in the Pythagorean and Platonic schools which accomplished illumination without the use of Oriental disciplines.

In substitution for the elaborate mechanism of Eastern spiritual culture are two simple disciplines, *meditation* and *realization.* By meditation a new sense of values and a clear perception of the relative worth of all knowledge are gained. By realization the student will make knowledge a part of his own life and consciousness. Through the practice of meditation and realization he gradually and normally will bring about the same results achieved in the East through more violent exercises. Natural growth, not forced growth, is the pattern to follow for the achievement of Truth.

SELF-ANALYSIS

A FRANK and honest estimation of your virtues and vices is absolutely necessary to spiritual growth. This inventory must be thorough but impersonal. When you have the debits and credits of character before you, you are in a position to balance your spiritual budget.

This analysis must not result in despair, self-depreciation, or an overwhelming sense of sin. Shortcomings require no more than a well-defined program of correction. A man full of the realization of his own sins is as far from Truth as a man filled with realization of his own virtues.

The old theological tradition that there is a certain virtue in stewing in one's own remorse has no place in mystical philosophy.

Perfection is reserved for the gods. It is not expected that the average person should live without fault or error, but it is most desirable that we profit by our mistakes. So never permit the mistakes of the past to overshadow present effort. The past must be transmuted into soul power through understanding. Do not bring forward separate incidents to plague your present purposes. Bring forward the sum of experience and understanding in the form of tolerance, patience, and virtue.

From the past we too often inherit a body of prejudices and inhibitions. Habits of thinking and living are not quickly changed, nor are prejudices of a lifetime easily dispelled. There is no use trying to go forward toward light and truth as long as we cherish destructive attitudes in our personal lives. Nearly everyone nurses some grievance or delinquency with loving care. Other faults are quickly remedied, other virtues are assiduously cultivated, but this one soft, sore spot is a sacred privilege which the gods must overlook. As one student said: "I am trying awful hard. Surely God won't mind if I continue disliking Henry. Didn't he steal from me everything I had? Hasn't he abused me ever since we were boys? God just can't ask me to forgive Henry after all the things he has done."

When you get your faults and failings all classified, and your virtues all arranged in their most flattering pattern, examine each of these products of your own consciousness with discriminating care and perceive wherein your own mind does not think straight. Observe carefully where the biases are, why the intemperances have been permitted, and most of all how these may be corrected justly and permanently. In examining this chart of your own ups and downs be particularly observant of extremes. One virtue rising majestically from the midst of numberless faults, or one vice holding forth tyrannically over many petty virtues, is the usual pattern.

It is far better to be moderately good in all things than to be outstandingly good in one thing and deficient in all the other virtues. Man is most nearly balanced when all his attitudes, ideals, and opinions are equally developed. An extreme unbalance frequently leads to mild forms of insanity not recognized pathologically, but nevertheless present to confound the soul.

Man has forty-three brain faculties. When one or two of these faculties are developed out of proportion to the rest, a form of vampirism results. The highly developed faculty draws to itself the blood and energy which should be evenly distributed. Thus, as any one faculty increases, the power of surrounding faculties are proportionately depleted. The one faculty is vampirizing the others.

A case is known of religious mania in which the brain faculty of veneration increased so greatly during years of fanaticism that the rest of the brain became comparatively inactive. An autopsy revealed that the bones of the skull over this highly developed area had become so thin that the surgeon punctured the skull with the point of a lead pencil. While one-pointedness is now called genius, and the narrow-minded have inherited the earth, it still remains philosophically true that narrow-mindedness is a disease, one-pointedness a menace to normalcy, and one exaggerated virtue the worst vice that a person can possess.

Self-analysis consists of sitting down quietly with a paper and pencil and making a personal inventory of the strength and weakness of each of the parts of your mental and emotional nature. Ten should be regarded as well-developed in grading any faculty or emotional reflex; zero for the complete absence; five would represent a half-developed faculty. Seven in any faculty is the norm for an intelligent person. As in most cases, there are one or two classifications to which you might give nine or ten; many will be comparatively undeveloped. Having completed your grading, which must be done with absolute honesty or it is worthless, you will then have a graph of yourself; that is, you will see yourself as the world knows you to be: the result of the things you think, feel, and do. The following list is to be used in making this analysis:

Estimate your *mental sufficiency* by grading yourself according to these ten classifications:

1. Continuity ____
2. Perseverance ____
3. Thoroughness ____
4. Tranquillity ____
5. Discrimination ____
6. Inclusiveness ____
7. Poise ____
8. Moderation ____
9. Detachment from results ____
10. Sense of humor ____

Estimate *emotional balance* from these ten classifications:

1. Personal harmony ____
2. Control of appetites ____
3. Control of affections ____

4. Control of fear ——
5. Control of worry ——
6. Control of enthusiasm ——
7. Development of artistic impulses ——
8. Friendliness ——
9. Temperance ——
10. Control of the tendency to venerate ——

Consider *bodily equilibrium* under these ten classifications:

1. Proper distribution of time, the assignment of appropriate periods for all physical action ——
2. Bodily health ——
3. Control of destructive bodily habits ——
4. Diet ——
5. Control of ornamentation and ostentation ——
6. Capitalization of bodily assets, by proper thoughtfulness for appearance and overcoming physical neglect ——
7. Exercise ——
8. Ventilation ——
9. Control of lost motion and confused action ——
10. Discipline of the body to obey the purposes of the will ——

SELF-CORRECTION

YOU are strongly urged to be thorough, honest, and impersonal in your self-analysis. When you realize fully your own faults, these faults are half-corrected. Few people have ever analyzed themselves, or been brought face to face with their own idiosyncrasies. Confront a problem, accept that problem as a personal responsibility, and solution is imminent. Self-analysis and self-correction will in themselves reward you for conscientious effort even if you should go no further in metaphysical disciplines. Only self-mastery through discipline can bring you temporal security and those good things of life which everyone desires.

After you have concluded your self-analysis examine carefully the graph which results. Consider your strongest points, that is, the virtues and abilities which dominate. Your problem now is to bring the rest of your mental and emotional attributes up to the same level, for it would be most detrimental to continue elevating your strong points.

Next look at the graph and observe the weakest of your characteristics. It is this characteristic which is binding you to a level far below that of normalcy. It is here that your self-improvement must begin.

You have already been told that aggressiveness must be taken out of self-discipline. It is possible to overcome any undesirable characteristic by what the Taoists call "effortless effort."

For example, if you have a bad temper there is only one way to overcome it: *stop having a bad temper*. An even temper is not accomplished by a magnificent gesture of the will, nor by a series of platitudinous affirmations, but by *realization*.

As you review your own life you may attempt to excuse your faults on the grounds of circumstances, feeling that conditions beyond your control are the true causes of mistakes made; much more in life would have been accomplished had fortune smiled.

Success and integrity are not matters of opportunity, but evolve in character. The noblest, wisest, and most virtuous of human beings are not those who have had the greatest opportunities. Those whose difficulties are numerous frequently develop the best philosophies of life; those whose problems are petty bewail their fate the loudest.

Not because the world has been good to them are Taoist monks happy. They are happy because they have been good to the world. They are philosophers who live moderate and virtuous lives, not for elaborate moral reasons but because it is easier and more pleasant to live well than it is to live any other way. Anger, fear, worry—these emotions are uncomfortable, and the Taoist is dedicated to comfort. Why should he make himself miserable when it is just as easy to be happy? These aged priests do not sit about on rocks with clenched teeth and high blood pressure trying to be good. They do not try to control their tempers. They are so well-tempered that temper is forgotten. They do not try to overcome selfishness. They have discovered the futility of the desire to possess. Nor are they trying to develop dominant personalities; they have not the slightest interest in what other people think of them. With this complete detachment and impersonality the Taoist monks frequently live to extreme old age. Their *realization* has so perfectly freed them from the irritations of physical existence that they are immune to most of the ailments which shorten the lives of Occidental people.

The accomplishment of the greatest good is the fundamental purpose of life. This accomplishment is hindered and frustrated by attachment to personalities and things. The moment we overestimate the value of material things we become incapable of a philosophical administration of the affairs of physical life. The moment we develop an undue attachment to persons we become incapable of serving them intelligently. It is a common, almost universal fault to develop undue attachments based upon the conceit that we are capable of possessing anything. The Taoist monk has made the pleasant discovery that he owns nothing; hence there is nothing about which he must worry or fear. Buddha taught that possession was one of the cardinal sins, and fatal to spiritual growth. The wise man is attached only to Principle, Universal Truth behind all things, and he possesses only the desire for Truth. This does not mean that he is selfish or inconsiderate of others. He serves all men impersonally because to him there is no distinction of family, nation, or race.

According to Pythagoras all relationships are based upon wisdom. On one occasion he is credited with saying: "He who is wiser than I is my father. He whose wisdom is equal to my own is my brother. And he who is of wisdom less than myself is my son." The universalizing of attachments and the impersonalizing of the sense of possession frees man from the great body of common sorrow.

POSITIVE FOUNDATIONS

HAVING clarified certain misconceptions common to many schools of popular metaphysics, we must now consider some of the positive virtues. Cultivation of these virtues is preparation for the life of wisdom; that is, a life dominated by reason and purpose. You cannot profit from metaphysical disciplines until you have created within yourself a capacity for them. This capacity must result from organization of faculties, stabilizing of emotions, and purposing of actions.

There must be a certain adequate foundation upon which to build the house of wisdom. When the King of Israel determined to build the Everlasting House he purchased the rock Moriah, which was the threshing floor of the Jebusites. This rock was an outcropping of azoic stone; a firm foundation that should endure forever.

A house can be no stronger than its foundations, nor a philosopher any wiser than the fundamentals of his doctrines. It has been taught by all schools of ancient religion that the spiritual development of the individual must be derived from a suitable foundation in virtue and integrity. A man is not necessarily virtuous merely because he possesses virtues. He is virtuous only when he administers these virtues wisely, with his mind free from conceits, prejudices, and errors. Integrity is not simply honesty; it is intelligent honesty. Wisdom is not only learning; it is enlightened learning. Mysticism not only investigates the subjective phenomena of life, but it develops an understanding and use of secret and sacred learning.

CONTINUITY

THE faculty of continuity is not highly developed in the average individual. The Western world as a whole is distinguished for its disconnectedness of effort; its general lack of thoroughness. Every student of the sacred sciences must realize that continuity and patience are absolutely necessary. Personal development requires years of conscientious, connected discipline. A person lacking patience should not even attempt the study of the sacred sciences.

Metaphysical impatience takes the form of wandering from one teacher to another and from one metaphysical system to another. Each new cult appears to promise a more speedy illumination, and the inconsistent neophyte finally degenerates into a roving cultist. This type of would-be Truth seeker has not the capacity for continuity. He hastens about from one infallible revelation to another, while his mental processes gradually deteriorate until he becomes incapable of intelligent thought.

Continuity is prosaically known as "stick-at-it-iveness." In the economic world, intelligent continuity of purpose is the greatest assurance of success. Our scintillating geniuses of finance, science, and industry, are nearly always men who have dedicated themselves to one purpose and have continued in that purpose until the desired end has been accomplished. The principal problem of the metaphysician is to develop a continuity that does not represent narrow-mindedness. To be tolerant in all things . . . to search for truth in all things . . . to recognize the good in all things . . . and at the same time to preserve perfect continuity of effort toward the development of self. *This* is a program which insures success.

Continuity does not arise from ignorance or lack of appreciation. The greater one's knowledge and the more diversified one's accomplishments, the more significant continuity becomes. Those who are not willing to devote a minimum of ten years to any well-authenticated system of development have no right to begin in the first place. They are certain to be disappointed, and probably will drift from one "ism" to another until death ends the drifting in this sphere.

Metaphysical development begins with continuity of discipline; and the struggle between continuity and interruption makes up our ordinary living. Continuity demands a sufficient will power to overcome interruption; a certain tenacity of purpose which will continue on unswervingly in the presence of what appears to be failure. No person who is true to the highest of his ideals can ultimately lose. Devotion to discipline and unswerving loyalty to truth and ideal will inevitably result in illumination. Only a mind and heart utterly devoted to the Real can finally be united with the Real.

THIRD REALIZATION

On one occasion Buddha discoursing to his disciples said: "I preach two doctrines—suffering, and the Law." The realization to be gained from this statement will assist the disciple in the important matter of self-orientation.

Living as we do in a world dominated largely by consequences of previous action, it is impossible to escape entirely from the complexities of karma. It is necessary, therefore, to accept the doctrine of suffering as an inevitable part of growth, and it is equally important that each incident of life should be meaningful, contributing something to the liberation of the Self.

Be thoughtful then in small things, especially in the inconsequential happenings which make up the day. Be observant in all that you do; seek to find the Law at work in all the diversified phases of living.

The keynote for this realization should be: FIND THE LAW! Seek for it in everything, everywhere, always. Become aware of the operations of universal causes in even the apparently trivial incidents. Remember the words of Michelangelo: "Trifles make perfection, and perfection is no trifle."

Observe the dignity of small matters. Learn the lessons to be derived from the contemplation of every useful and necessary action. Find the Law in work and in play, waking and sleeping; observe its functioning in the arts and crafts, sciences and professions. Realize that true education is to find the Law. Experience is only useful when the individual finds the true reason for the incident. Objects seen, customs practiced, and books studied result in merit only to the degree that through these experiences we find the Law.

Law everywhere manifesting through everything, perfecting all things in and through itself . . . meditate upon this mystery; unite your own mind with the purposed thinking of Space. In all your comings and goings, in your joys and sorrows, in your gains and losses, FIND THE LAW!

IV

PLACIDITY

PLACIDITY is inner harmony; a conscious realization of the rightness of life and law. Placidity when achieved conserves energy, prevents sickness, and prepares the consciousness for esoteric disciplines.

Placidity arises from the realization of the absolute rightness of the universe as it is; the absolute justice which directs the activities of all the forces which make up the life of the universe. No one is suffering for the sins of another; no one is in a place which he has not earned for himself; no one deserves more than he has; and no one should be happy who is not.

Happiness comes from within and is the result of spiritual unfoldment; the creature who does not possess that unfoldment cannot be happy. There is no one in the universe who has never had a chance. There is no one who is a victim of the machinations of others. There is no one who has had more adversities than he has earned. And there is no one who can escape his just rewards.

One of the principal causes of internal stress is the thought wasted worrying for other people; trying to live their lives and save them from their just deserts. A human being cannot be helped to escape from an experience necessary to him. And so there is very little use in trying to protect people from themselves; from the experiences that they need in order to grow. This realization will contribute definitely to the placidity of thousands of people who waste their time worrying about others.

Competitive metaphysics also is detrimental to placidity. The man worrying about his soul growth, or the one fretting inwardly because he has not yet had visions and initiations, is destroying the very environment required for inward enlightenment. It is as necessary to be detached from self as from the affairs of others.

The perception of these facts in the presence of personal misfortunes affecting ourselves and those for whom we care—*that is difficult*. But Law is immutable and absolutely just. Misfortunes which afflict those for whom we care are as just as those evils which afflict strangers and so-called enemies.

POISE

POISE is placidity manifested outwardly through a relaxed and ordered personality. Poise cannot be cultivated successfully merely by copying the actions of others. It has been attempted, but the appearance is not effective unless it arises from an adequate inward placidity. Poise is an evidence of internal equilibrium. It is proof that the excesses of attitude have died out in the individual as the result of practicing and living the mystical life.

The value of poise lies in its relaxing effect. Any inordinate emotion or tension arising in the subjective nature will destroy poise. Poise, being destroyed, reacts upon the entire organism—objective and subjective—to its detriment. This is another evidence that self-discipline not only improves the spiritual nature but is necessary to physical well-being.

Hence it should be your purpose to build so firm a foundation of integrity within yourself that the possibility of losing the inner vision that comes with poise becomes constantly less and less. In every case you should remedy the inner causes instead of laboring with the outer manifestations. If the inside is right, the outside is bound to be right. The test of philosophy comes with the observation of how far it has been able to lift you above the pettiness of personality into the realm of universals.

INCONSISTENCY

SPIRITUAL ideals and material faults cannot exist together in one body without ultimately destroying that body. It is not possible to gratify the destructive impulses of the animal nature and at the same time practice occult disciplines. Such inconsistency is rewarded with sickness and misery. Occult disciplines refine the body. The animal appetites render the body more coarse. Refinement and coarseness cannot abide together in the same organism without destroying the integrity of that organism. The spiritual sciences require mental and emotional consistency. Hence extremes in all things must die out with a realization of the Law *to the point of application.*

Closely related to the inconsistencies of action is the imperiousness of desire. The common belief is that the only thing which will make us happy is to receive something we have desired. Whether we have earned it does not worry us. Many who intellectually affirm the law of cause and effect—"As ye sow so shall ye reap"—within themselves are hopeful to the end that exceptions will be made. Students are anxious to welcome the rewards of karma, but still rebel against misfortunes and consider them mistakes on the part of the universe. To pray for that which is not our own and yet to say that we believe in the law of karma, is a hopeless contradiction that destroys the unity of our purpose.

PATIENCE

PATIENCE is an attitude that develops with the realization that in the fullness of time the Law brings to pass that which is right. The speed at which we learn is not important. A great Brahman sage once said that the universe is so constructed that no matter how slowly we grow, we shall always have time to grow. If it takes a hundred million years for man to gain one idea, the universe has a hundred million years—and it will wait for man. Man is not pushed to accomplishment; each individual will have the time necessary to grow. But the wise do not take all the time there is; they start to work on themselves with an increasing realization of the Law.

Overestimation of self is a common cause of impatience. Man's idea of optimism is expressed in the hope that he is more highly developed than he really is, and so should have more of light, understanding, happiness, peace, and security than he enjoys. But there are no oversights on the part of Providence. No individual is an exile from his own reward. If man deserved one thing more than he has, he would have it. Lack is due to the individual's oversight in failing to be anything or to earn anything.

Only the highest type of mankind has the patience to perform a given task for a hundred lifetimes without deviating for a moment from his goal. It is those who possess this integrity who realize Truth.

DIRECTNESS OF ACTION

THE purpose of energy is to enliven all parts of nature; to supply the very essence of achievement—life itself. Most people pay little attention to their energy allotment. They waste energy indiscriminately until it is gone and then they wonder why the universe has afflicted them. The serious studies of the metaphysician usually begin after he has reached those years when energy is not too abundant. The exuberance of youth is over, toil and responsibility have exacted their toll, and it is necessary to organize resources and conserve all life for the principal purpose of living and enlightenment.

The Taoist monk will do nothing that is not absolutely necessary. He would no more think of stalking in the hills than brawling on the street corner. He is principally concerned with conserving his energy so that he will possess it long enough to achieve enlightenment. Because of his very moderate attitude he enjoys good health in his advanced years, and usually dies of old-age rather than from one of the forms of unintentional suicide which exterminate Occidentals.

Directness of action means the doing of a thing by the simplest and most direct means; living by the simplest and most direct codes; fulfilling all responsibilities in the simplest and most direct ways; and applying principle to the various problems of life directly and simply, without sentiment, prejudice, or opinion.

When the task is finished one should let go mentally and physically, returning to his composure until the next duty of life presents itself. Life is not a series of fractional circumstances each out of perspective with the rest, even though many lives appear like erratic actions on a film, with mental lapses between.

For those who work in harmony with the Law, life is an inward flowing picture that moves placidly from one thing to another. There are no interruptions because there are no accidents in the universe, and every incident in life is significant. Instead of living the thousand and one incidents of life you will live one life in which the thousand and one incidents are bound together; so bound that everything which happens is right — not because you blindly ignore that which apparently is not right but because you will have found a more inclusive rightness that encompasses all life.

You will find that you can move through the day unmoved by whatever happens. Events will achieve their relative importance. All experiences become lessons to be welcomed. Everything that occurs becomes part of a well-ordered process. Things which make foolish men angry make evident the poise of the wise. Suffering is not a matter of what happens to us but a matter of how we take the thing that happens—enriched when accepted with inner realization.

The same realization is true of death, which to many is a great interruption to the purposes of life. To the philosopher life and death are parts of a greater living. Living in the presence of the inevitable there is no place for regret, but only for balanced acceptance.

This realization will help you in your business, home, and relationships with people. Whether you go on to other metaphysical disciplines, the fact remains that you can live only when you can extricate your consciousness from the particular mistakes you make every day. If you can find wisdom and mental integrity; if you honestly can say to yourself, "People have lost the power to hurt me; circumstances can no longer obscure convictions of principle"; then you can achieve an inner quiet. When you can stop the rising of thoughts, and have found placidity and peace, you can be still enough to feel universal life flowing through you. You can be quiet enough to hear the "Voice of the Silence." You can be inwardly so at peace and so utterly placid that the quiet and calm of your consciousness will enable you to hear the mantras of the Law.

All of this inward consciousness is evidenced by peace in the outer nature. He who has not achieved this peace can never find God. The conquest is the nondestructive, nonaggressive attainment of realization, poise, detachment—the *Posture of the Law.*

SYMBOLS OF REALIZATION

THE East Indian schools of occult philosophy give special attention to postures, mudras, and mantras. Postures mean bodily positions associated with forms of meditation and breathing. Postures are most numerous in the Tantric, Buddhist, and Yoga schools. Some of the body postures are exceedingly difficult to assume and require years of practice. Their principal purpose is to control the direction of energy flowing into the body from the earth, the elements, and the celestial bodies.

Mudras are hand-patterns, positions assumed by the fingers in the performance of certain symbolical rituals.

The study of the mudras also includes the technique of holding, picking up, and setting down sacred instruments such as bells, wands, and the *dorje*. The mudras have reached their highest degree of perfection among the Buddhist priests of Ceylon. They also occur in Tibet, where the various deified Buddhist saints and princes are represented in certain postures as they perform appropriate mudras.

The mantra is a form of chanting, which occurs in nearly all religions. The virtue of the mantra lies in the sounding of certain syllables, the sounds setting up vibratory vortices. Most ancient peoples acknowledged the significance of sound, and used various mantras in the invocation of their gods and in propitiating their deified ancestors. In India the mantra is said to purify the body by its vibratory power, at the same time stimulating the chakras or nerve centers.

It must be evident to the profound metaphysical student that posture, mudra, and mantra are of symbolic rather than literal significance. This point has been emphasized by the Zen monks, who insist that all physical ceremonials are symbolic of mystic processes taking place within man himself. The Greeks held a similar opinion; also the fathers of the early Christian Church. But the mystical aspects of ritualism have been gradually forgotten; now the various ceremonies are supposed to possess intrinsic powers, sacred in their effects.

Sincere students are warned against the dangers of ritualistic entanglements. The modern religious world is full of formulas. While these formulas have their place (as shadows of facts), it is presumed that the true mystic has outgrown the necessity of participating in religious fables. Every type of formula from the "Om" formula of the Hindus to the "peace, power, and plenty" affirmation of popular psychology belong to a type of ritualism which can be very detrimental if accepted as the substance of reality.

Yet it cannot be denied that there are "words of power." Also that certain rituals have a magical effect. But the modern metaphysician is not sufficiently informed to dabble in magic. It is unnecessary to his spiritual development. As the great transcendental magician Eliphas Levi admitted, it can easily become a blind alley.

As all mudras and mantras are exceedingly dangerous for the inexperienced, being in the same class as the chakra development exercises and the yoga breathing exercises, such disciplines have been carefully eradicated from the teachings of these pages, in full agreement with the Zen teachings that they are not necessary to spiritual development, do not represent the essence of Truth, and belong to the paraphernalia of cults.

POSTURE

THE ancient books tell us, and so too the most venerable of the *gurus,* that a disciple preparing to practice meditation, or any of the metaphysical disciplines, must first master the posture or body arrangement which accompanies the discipline. The postures are positions of trained relaxation. The informed gurus know that these postures are only symbolical of inner conditions of consciousness; the actual position of the body is comparatively irrelevant, but the mental discipline of each posture is extremely important.

When it is said that the sannyasin "seats" himself, you must realize that the "seating" posture is an inner, mystical experience rather than a physical position. You must think of the mind as being disciplined, not the body.

To "seat" oneself is to rest firmly in the Law, to establish one's consciousness rightly in the sphere of universal values. To "seat" oneself in the Law is to place one's realization in the eternal, never-changing, ever-real Law of life. It is recognition of the absolute integrity of the universe, the absolute truth of Reality. When the Buddhist monk says, "I put my faith in the Law," he means that he posits his consciousness in the reality of Supreme Rightness. He has found his own center of consciousness in the realization of the rightness of things as they are. Realizing the significance of his present estate, and relieved of vain hopes, he turns constructively to improvement through right action, and to earning that which is necessary.

Most of the ancient teachers taught while sitting down, frequently on a knoll or low hill, with their disciples gathered about them. Statues of Buddha and his arhats (saints) usually depict the master seated on the open petals of a lotus with his hands in the mudra of instruction.

Many of the scriptural books begin with such a phrase as "the master seated himself." This establishment, or taking refuge in the Law, signifies that the disciple has completed his searching. He no longer travels from sage to sage begging wisdom. He has become aware that Truth is within and that he no longer need search for it in place, but within himself. He has discovered peace within. He has discovered that his own being is the axis of the universe. He neither questions nor doubts the integrity of the doctrines he has followed; he is certain as to the essential principles of his philosophy. This conviction, this final acceptance of Truth as Reality, is called "establishment in the Law."

Most modern Truth seekers have wandered far afield searching for the answer to life's questions. They have knocked at many doors and have received many answers. They have been exploited and deceived. Their faith in human nature has been strained. And all for the one reason—they did not know that Truth was within.

In the search they receive many answers, much knowledge, but not Truth. Like Buddha, wandering from holy man to holy man, they must finally realize that the end of all searching, of all rites and rituals, of all symbols and allegories, is the realization of indwelling reality.

To be "seated" in the Law, one, like the meditating Buddha, must be in a condition of absolute integrity. There must be absolute poise, absolute tranquillity, absolute peace. Having achieved this condition the disciple is ready to receive further instruction. Reserving no part of himself, living with no purpose of his own, demanding nothing, he awaits the fulfillment of the Law within himself. This is the end of egotism, the final dying out of the fires of emotion and desire. This complete at-one-ment with the Law brings the only security of which man is capable. Then, truly, the disciple is "seated" in the Law.

Bodhidharma, according to tradition, crossed the China Sea on a floating palm leaf. The storms raged and the waves rose, and the thunder of the sea was like the sounds of war. But a pathway of calm opened in the midst and the Buddhist patriarch wrapped in his green cloak traveled safely through the sea on his magic leaf. This legend has a significance similar to that of the biblical account of Jesus walking on the waters.

Thus is realization symbolized: The sea is life. The sea, ruffled by every wind that blows upon its surface, is the mind of man, moved by every breath of emotion and opinion, churned by the storms of the worries and terrors of the day. Yet in the midst of this stormy sea of life the arhat walks along a pathway of calm—because he is immovable in his realization of the Law.

Compare such an estate with the troublous life most mortals lead. Compare the worries and fears that afflict the flesh with this peaceful detachment, this security, this absolute sufficiency. Remember the story of Buddha: As a young prince he saw sickness and sorrow and death; and then he beheld a monk, a quiet-faced man of gentle mien who walked slowly down the dusty road unmoved and unattached, and Buddha decided immediately that it was better to be like that man than to rule the kingdoms of the earth. Such is *establishment;* such is truly a secure foundation. Upon the open petals of the lotus, the symbol of enlightenment, sits the sage; sustained by his own realization, immovable, "seated" in the Law.

BECOMING IMMOVABLE

BECOMING immovable in the Law does not mean a rigor of the body, but is symbolic of a fundamental integrity of purpose. The disciple must accept some system of discipline and stay with it. He must set himself so securely with a one-pointed purpose that neither the element of time nor any material interruption can shift him from his purpose.

We must realize that our approach to the Real is in the integrity of ourselves. The neophyte, before entering meditation, closes the circuits of himself. In the old books

MULTIPLICATION OF THE PATTERNS. THE STUDENT REALIZES DIVISION WITHIN HIMSELF BUT IS NOT DIVIDED. THE ONE IS REALIZED IN ITS THREE BASIC MODES OR QUALITIES. THESE ARE THE ROOTS OF THE EXTENSIONS OF CONSCIOUSNESS WITHIN THE SELF

showing the pictures of meditating philosophers we find the body formed into a figure "8" by the crossing of the hands and feet. There are two reasons for this. The first is to close out contrary vibratory forces. The second is to prevent the scattering of vibratory forces.

Shutting off all undesirable forces actually means that the individual by realization causes levels of action, thoughts, and emotions which are lower than himself, to die out of his own consciousness. Excluding outside evils is exclusion of the inferiority of personality. "Outside" in the metaphysical sense does not always mean the external environment as much as the body which is outside of Self. The cutting off of outside things means the conscious lifting of the mind to a level where mental and emotional factors die out. Achieving the higher level the disciple is no longer troubled with the interferences of consciousness, at least during the period of meditation.

The "closing in" of vital forces means that the individual shall in all things conserve himself; for no one can achieve a high degree of spiritual accomplishment who scatters his resources. We must remember that meditation and realization use for their fulfillment the same energy that is used for all the occupations and concerns of life.

The problem of conserving energy and reserving energy, of not wasting it through any thought or action, is an important one. Not one ounce of vitality which is necessary for the extension of the mind should be wasted. It is in the holding of the hands and feet in a certain position that we have the symbol of this preservation of energy.

Unselfishness of purpose is signified by the lifting up of the body from the earth so that the currents of the earth will not rise through the spinal base. This yoga practice means dissociation of purpose—by mental energy—because that which belongs to the inner life must not be debased or perverted by being involved in material accomplishment. It must be separate from all irrational extremes.

DISCIPLINE

THE foundation has now been laid for the general practice of discipline. Indicated at least have been a group of special ways in which, through a better standard of thinking and a higher level of understanding we can improve the whole life. That general improvement is vital to the achievement of specific results.

Specific exercises are prepared for individual purposes. The problem of this book has been the devising of a series of exercises of gradually unfolding disciplines which would be safe to give to a large number of people. All Yoga, Tantric, and Buddhist disciplines are individual in application. It is impossible to give one Yoga discipline that will be helpful to five people in the same group. It will be harmful to four of the five, if not actually fatal.

Everyone needs some form of metaphysical discipline, and yet circumstances make it impossible to examine individually into the needs of all people. The problem is clarified by the application of the Law itself, namely: While all things are different and separate, finally all things are one, having a common nature as their cause. Or, as Plato says, "All specifics are suspended from generals."

The problem has been to devise a system which can produce only good, and which will protect itself in several ways. It will protect itself against those who would use it to gain results in a brief time. The individual who lacks the integrity to use it will not have the patience to follow it.

In the simple system developed, no elaborate posture is necessary. It is not so important how an individual sits or holds his hands, as that posture should conform with discipline. You should not be entirely comfortable, nor should there be an absolute lack of comfort. Absolute comfort generally leads to sleep in occult disciplines. Working with faculties little used, the first impulse is to go to sleep. No exercise should be performed in bed.

Many people have marvelous poise until they are interrupted in one of their exercises. Then they are not slow in expressing their irritation. In meditation be prepared to meet interruption happily. Anyone who is irritated by interruptions is too sensitive in a negative sense to achieve positive results. No matter how many interruptions occur a wise person cannot be interrupted, due to the fact that he is ready at all times to get up and do the necessary thing. With complete poise and inward peace achieved, you can pass through the numerous vicissitudes that upset most people without any sense of interruption.

In the beginning the efforts of the disciple are in a feeble state. It is thus better to have a quiet place for meditation, protected from unnecessary interruption; there is no advantage in increasing the hazards in the infant stages of development. In a more advanced state the student will be taken out of the secret place. He will put himself on the street corner, for the purpose is not to overcome peace, but discord. To overcome the discord in living, the individual in meditation should be able to relegate the most unpleasant sounds to their proper places in the universal harmony. The wise man cannot be interrupted, nor will he hear discord in the atmosphere around him. Meditating between a trolley car and a train, the noise of both will not interrupt him.

Next to be considered is the chair, or whatever type of seat is going to be used. The exercise should be taken, preferably, sitting in a straight but comfortable chair. The chair should not be overstuffed, permitting you to collapse in it; on the other hand, it should not be a bony, unpleasant thing. Life is a balance between comforts and discomforts, so the chair chosen should be a symbol of life, moderately comfortable, but one that makes you sit up. Chairs that hold out arms embracingly are too much like false doctrines.

It is important that this same seat or chair be used for the first six months. After that it should intentionally be discarded because you must be able to accomplish meditation anywhere, under any condition.

The meditation exercises must not be coddled. On the other hand they should not be made unnecessarily difficult until some degree of strength is acquired. Like the small child, the neophyte must learn to crawl before he can walk.

Regularity of discipline is most important. Choose some hour that is the common denominator of the quiet hours of the day, either before you have begun your business for the day or after you have finished your activities. Choose a time not likely to be changed. If necessary, choose some unusual hour—but not so unusual that it is on your mind all the time or you will probably not forget it during meditation. Also see to it that you do not have more than one breaking of the sequence within a week—at least six days out of seven keep your appointment with yourself.

After you have chosen the seat and the time, and have prepared a suitable environment within yourself, you must bear in mind that you begin in peace and end in the turmoil of life. You begin by yourself, but in the end you must learn to meditate among all men. You begin in comfort, but gradually you must learn to meditate amidst discomfort. You train yourself in order and rhythm so that you can do that for a few seconds which later you will be able to do at all times and any time. You will be taking a few feeble steps to something that will gradually absorb your life and give it great richness.

FOURTH REALIZATION

Your fourth realization: LISTEN FOR THE LAW. Ponder well the meaning of the words. Seek to discover that which cannot be written, but must be experienced.

As the singing lohans (Buddhist arhats) sang the Law in the Diamond Mountains of Korea, so the modern disciple must listen to the SONG OF TRUTH that is forever flowing through the worlds.

To hear the Law one must become silent, truly silent. Outer sound must be silenced. The inner ear must hear the CHANT OF SPACE.

Let the mind be still; let the desires be silent; let the body be relaxed; let all the senses and impulses be hushed—and thus LISTEN. In moments of stress, when problems threaten, when all life seems out of key—LISTEN.

If you have achieved the proper posture (mood), if you have placed yourself in the Law, you will hear. In the words of an Eastern poet: "The Law will come to you like the murmur of a summer breeze at eventide.

You will hear it like the sound of a soft breath flowing among the fronds of a palm tree." It is thus that you should understand the true meaning of the Biblical words that in the cool of the evening, the Lord (Law) walked in the garden.

In the midst of your living and in the midst of the problems of your living—LISTEN FOR THE LAW.

From *Illustrated Actions of the Sakyamuni Buddha on Persuading All the People.*
Yung Shan. 1808
THE MOTION OF REALITY, HERE REPRESENTED IN DRAGON FORM, ARISING IN THE CONSCIOUSNESS OF THE BUDDHA DURING MEDITATION

V

CONCENTRATION

FROM the realization of the esoteric significance of posture as establishment in the Law, we now proceed to the practice of the first of the seven operative disciplines. For convenience we term this first discipline *concentration.*

Concentration—and it is necessary to understand the meaning of the word in its truly mystical sense—is the gathering together of the faculties of the mind; it is the achievement of one-pointedness of purpose. As we use the word, concentration is best described in the terms of the Eastern adepts, "The master, seating himself, gathered his robes about him and entered samadhi."

"Seating himself" is understood to mean the posture or establishment. "Gathered his robes about him," indicates that he united or bound together, or drew to a point, the various faculties of the reason. This, then, is the true *doctrine of the mean.*

Reflect on the mystery of the gathering of the garments of wisdom. The Buddhist patriarchs were distinguished by their mantles. The various arhats or masters of the schools wore capes, the colors differing with each order. The mantle of Zen was green, and Daruma, the arhat of

Zen, is depicted totally wrapped in the folds of his mantle, one end of which is thrown over his head to form the hood. The disciples were not permitted to wear such cloaks, as they were the distinctive symbols of the superior abbots.

The Pythagorean initiate, Apollonius of Tyana, possessed a peculiar woolen cape. When he desired to practice the esoteric disciplines, he seated himself in the midst of this cape and drew it about him, covering even his face. While thus concealed he is supposed to have made magical journeys to distant parts of the world. It was while in one of these periods of superphysical extension that he saw at a great distance the assassination of the Emperor Domitian.

So long have we accepted symbols as realities that few students ever ask the meaning of the magical cloaks. These, like the enchanted carpet of Bagdad, Solomon's magic ring, and the ring of the Nibelungs, are symbols of concentration—the gathering up and the pointing together of the faculties of the mind.

How then shall we define concentration? Like every other true discipline, its real meaning cannot be written. It must be perceived inwardly. It must be known because of the discipline having evolved within the disciple the understanding necessary to its practice. No physical cloak, of course, is required; the master is clothed in garments not of this world. The peculiarities of his physical raiment (by which his station is known in the physical world) are merely the shadows or emblems of his true dignities.

Concentration is gentle, unstrained, effortless one-pointedness. It is grounded and founded in the realization of the Law. It may be interpreted as *steadfastness* of purpose. As a candle burning in a still night, so is realization burning steadfastly in the midst of concentration.

Concentration is the continuity of spiritual motion toward the One. It is described in the commentaries on the Zohar thus: "The disciple of spiritual mysteries gazes with perfect fixedness of attention upon the face of the Real."

The simple practice of concentration is an entirely harmless discipline so long as false interpretation is prevented. But there is a great interval of understanding between the true practice of concentration and the popular misconceptions which have gained widespread acceptance.

PREPARATION FOR CONCENTRATION

NO occult discipline should be practiced without adequate preparation. In practice, preparation is of two kinds. The first form is concerned with the general state of individual living. It is useless to attempt any occult exercises in a contradictory and chaotic environment. You must not develop the attitude of fleeing from worldliness into a spiritual condition. Concentration is not an oasis of spirituality in a desert of chaos.

So often people say: "My daily meditation gives me the strength to go on in a life that otherwise would be too difficult." With such a motivation failure is inevitable. Concentration cannot be an incident in the midst of contrary incidents. It must be intimately correlated to the whole pattern of living or it will not succeed, and the time devoted to the effort will be wasted.

In the life of man the power to concentrate, according to the mystical meaning of the word, is evidence of an increasing internal poise and the extension of soul power through life as it is daily lived. Hence the first part of concentration is related to the general pattern of the disciple's degree of understanding.

The second part of the preparation is that phase which immediately precedes the actual practice of the discipline. For a short time prior to a period devoted to concentration the mind should be in a condition of repose, and there should be a complete physical relaxation—not necessarily idleness, but an entire absence of stress. To sit down in the midst of confusion and try suddenly and forcibly to block it out by means of an attitude is unreasonable and unphilosophical. It is for this reason that the master first "seats himself." These few words define a great mystery for those who can comprehend.

CONCENTRATION SYMBOLS

THE priesthood of antiquity and the mystical institutions of modern Asia are in perfect agreement as to the use of various sacred objects in the practice of concentration. Pythagoras taught his disciples to meditate upon the mystery of the tetractys, a triangular arrangement of ten dots. He also advised all genuine Pythagoreans to devote time to the realization of the peculiar sacredness of the dodecahedron or twelve-sided symmetrical solid. Plutarch, in his *Mysteries of Isis and Osiris,* declared that the Egyptians concealed within the adyta of their temples mysterious geometrical forms and patterns, the contemplation of which inspired toward a proximity with the gods. Theon of Smyrna, the mathematician, advocated that Deity be attained as a state through the contemplation of the patterns of numbers according to a regular progression. A considerable part of religious art and architecture belonging to the old mystery cults was actually involved in the practice of their contemplation disciplines. When so understood, the old symbols take on a new dignity and a richer meaning.

The modern Lama makes use of several symbolical instruments in the performance of his mystical rituals. These include the dorje or double thunderbolt, the ceremonial dagger, the bowl, a small two-headed drum, the mandala, the prayer wheel, and the tanka. To these objects must be added the elaborate imagery which makes up the Tibetan pantheon. Each of the divinities represented is depicted in certain postures and performing certain actions. To the initiated each of these subtle variations has special esoteric significance.

Among the concentration formulas of the Chinese Taoists, the word *Tao* itself occupies the chief place. Next in importance is the ying-yang symbol, representing the equilibrium of the positive-negative poles. Following in importance is the pattern of trigrams, groups of whole and broken lines of which there are recognized eight primary and sixty-four secondary combinations. The commentary by Confucius on the esoteric mysteries of the trigram formulas is held in the highest veneration.

Calligraphy contributes to the concentration symbols of both the Chinese and Japanese. Involved written characters embodying certain principles of form, line, and rhythm are regarded as especially efficacious. Religious paintings, sculpturings, and frescoes adorn most Eastern temples. They also are part of the religious life of the devout. The paintings most widely admired are the work of priests who execute symbolical designs while they are in a state of meditation. All beautiful and meritorious works of artists and craftsmen are regarded as possessing the power to stimulate inner realization.

Such is the exoteric doctrine in regard to concentration symbols. Even some of the more mystical sects accept the literal sanctity of these objects. For our purposes, however, we must search more deeply for the true *Tao,* that is, for the right *Way* to the understanding of the sacred symbols.

Each of the emblems symbolizes and represents a function of the mind, a condition of the Self, or expression of the will. They are, therefore, pictures or physical likenesses of the invisible formulas of truths, virtues, or states. By truth is meant reality; by virtue, likeness to fact; and by state, the level or degree of proximity to reality. Here again, only realization itself can clearly distinguish between terms that in popular usage have been accepted as practical synonyms. In mysticism all meanings are subtle, and the most subtle are the most nearly true.

When it is written that the master picks up the dorje it means that he is grasping universal power within his consciousness, balancing cosmic energies by the process of concentration. When he elevates the dagger he is cutting the bond of sense. When he holds the bowl he is receptive to the inflowing of universals. When he spins the wheel he is turning the truths of cause and effect upon the axis of the Self. Thus it is with each instrument in turn. No actual or physical symbol is necessary or implied. The tangible remains as it always must, merely the key or clue to the mystery of the intangible. To the uninitiated many of these truths must remain obscure and meaningless. Thus the secrets protect themselves by their very nature, and cannot be profaned by the unworthy. Those who have not eyes to see have not the skill to use or the power to abuse.

MANDALA MAGIC

THE mandala is a sacred painting or diagram usually symmetrical and geometrical rather than pictorial. The size is of little consequence, and the colorings, though often traditional, vary considerably. The complete arrangement may be basically lotus-form, and the compartments or symbolic petals may be ornamented with Chinese, Tibetan, or Sanskrit letters or numbers. Exoterically the mandala is a kind of universe map depicting the symbolic form of the world, the heavens, the paradisiacal abodes or symbolical parts of the human body.

While the conventionalized form of the mandala is recognized throughout Asia, various sects have created definite departures from the traditional type. Only an advanced disciple thoroughly familiar with the mystical disciplines can identify with certainty all types of the mandala. Also, he alone can discriminate between the genuine temple formulas and the commercial reproductions which unscrupulous art dealers prepare to deceive and exploit the tourist trade.

The celebrated Abbe Huc was unfrocked by his church after he had published reports about certain magical rites practiced in the innermost parts of Asia. One among other interesting observations was the learned Abbe's comment on a mandala painting he discovered in one of the temples. A design on the painting included a figure representing the moon. The painted symbol, according to the Abbe's report, changed on the canvas, conforming exactly to the phases of the moon in the sky.

There is considerable literature available in the Far East which explains such magic painting to those capable of understanding. For example, one legend is of the Buddhist monk who painted (while in a state of raptured meditation) the gate of Sukhavati, the door to the Western heaven of Amitabha. His masterpiece completed, he hung the silken painting upon the wall of his cell. One day while deep in meditation he rose, stepped over to the painting, walked through the gate he himself had painted, and disappeared forever. He had attained Nirvana.

How to interpret this legend? If we depend upon the faculties of the mind alone, the story seems strange and absurd. If, however, we possess the power to contemplate the true mystery of the legend, it becomes a sublime allegory. The meditating monk is the Self imprisoned within the human form which represents the limitations of the mortal mind. The painting is the visualization of the "middle road," the *tao*. The picture represents a gate or door because it truly is the "way." Having through concentration visualized and participated in the mystery of the right "way," the disciple is able to attain the end which, like the way, is *tao*. The Truth is reached through his own realization; he becomes one with that which he has realized. Concentration is the gateway to the Real; the bridge built of the subtle stuff of the inwardly perceived. He who builds the bridge may pass across it to identity with that which he has built.

Young disciples in some of the Eastern schools are set to the task of concentrating daily upon the mandala patterns. They are then questioned as to the results they have achieved. Usually the first experience is the sensing that the patterns move. If the mandala be wheel-like it appears to revolve, first slowly and later with a gradually increasing velocity until the colors mingle and seem to become whirling disks of light. The attainment of such results requires many months—sometimes years—of daily concentration.

In the next stage the background of the painting, the wall upon which it is hung, and all other surrounding objects slowly disappear, and the whirling disk is seen hanging in space supported only by the power of concentration.

In the third stage the concentrating disciple feels himself and the disk drawn together, experiencing the sensation of flowing into a vortex of luminous power. When this condition is reached the disciple must appeal to his teacher for assistance before proceeding further. He is at the forking of the road. A mistake at this point may undo all the work of years of effort.

The master then interrogates the disciple as to what he has discovered by the whirling of the disk. The purpose of the questioning is to find out whether the concentration is essentially visual or truly mystical. If it is visual only, the symbol is taken away; otherwise the results verge toward idolatry. Metaphysically, idolatry means to mistake the symbol for the Real; to worship the symbol as Reality. If the disciple's experience has been primarily a mechanical one and he has seen the whirling disk as he might gaze at some object outside of himself, he has failed.

His concentration must have caused him to EXPERIENCE the wheel. He must have found it as a value, not a form. It must be a living wheel, the very Law itself in motion. The master will ask for an explanation of the true meaning of the whirling mandala. If the disciple replies that he knows but cannot explain; if the master sees in the eye of the disciple the light of soul power and perceives in every gesture the awakened strength of realization, he will be satisfied. By certain occult means of penetration the teacher can accurately estimate the advancement that has been made. If it is satisfactory, certain instruction is given and the disciple told to proceed. He is given the thunderbolt and told to smash the wheel. He must destroy the pattern of his own concentration, and he must do this while in concentration. Beyond this point words cannot go.

For the novice, therefore, the key is this: concentration is the envisionment of the Law through magical or transcendental forms. Law is found in the form. The form however, must be broken up. The Law is formless. It can be found through form, but never in form. All forms, tangible and intangible, reveal the Law. Woe to him who attempts to catch the Law within the net of mind! . . . Such is the introduction to mandala magic.

THE BEGGING BOWL

THE principal symbol of discipleship is the begging bowl. This circular vessel of bronze or clay is the badge of mendicancy, the emblem of nonpossession. But it should not infer moral indigence. Like the other sacred relics of arhatship, it must be realized as an experience of the consciousness. The principal architectural motif of the Shwe Dagon Pagoda, one of the most impressive of all Buddhist shrines, is an inverted begging bowl. The inverted bowl itself as the reliquary of the liberated adept tells one of the deepest of universal secrets.

The search for Truth is an experience of the part searching for wholeness. It is a discipline of acceptance.

Although the term "seeking" is the best we know, truly we do not seek Truth. We accept, we receive, yet we do not find. All that lives and exists bestows something. Reality is forever flowing in and through all that is. The bowl is a symbol of the mental capacity to receive. Hence the devout Buddhist may accept in it only that which is necessary for a single day—and nothing but food. Rice is the bread of Asia. The Christian in his prayer exclaims: "Give us this day our daily bread." The Buddhist mystic does not even ask. He carries the bowl and those who feel within the impulse of the good Law will share their rice with him.

When food is offered the mendicant may not refuse it. It is told of the Buddha Gautama that on his last day upon the earth a poor farmer out of the generosity of his heart put into the Buddha's bowl a portion of his food. Due to the poverty of the giver the food was spoiled. But the Enlightened One received it and turning to his disciples declared that the time had come for his departure from among them. Then, knowing that the food was tainted but the best that the poor man had to give, he gravely ate it, and died a short time after.

The story is obviously allegorical, but the meaning is perfectly clear. To receive the Law is to be fed. Through all that lives the Law is brought to us, and in any case and under any circumstance we may receive the Law and achieve liberation. The experiences of the day, the problems of life, karma, and dharma, all must be accepted into the ever-open bowl of the consciousness. No lesser object than food is permissible, but who shall declare what is or what is not food? At the end, experience is perfected in Law. The one who has attained liberation turns the bowl over. When the Law is perfected, then the time of receiving is passed. Until then, the monk in his yellow robe wanders up and down the world carrying the bowl.

THE PRACTICE OF CONCENTRATION

READ over several times—thoughfully—this section, giving special attention to possible double meanings. These cannot always be pointed out or the discipline itself will fail.

The practice of concentration should be limited to a brief period, with special attention to regularity and continuity. If realization cannot be achieved by adjustment, the extension of the discipline is worthless. The disciple should concentrate for not more than five or ten minutes at any one time, once daily. Truth is timeless. The advisable daily period then, is five minutes, a number mystically associated with the control of the five sensory perceptions. Either mornings or evenings are suitable times. The middle of the day or night is less favorable, especially in the case of the novice. Day and night are the yin and yang; between them are the suitable times.

The time, the place, and the chair having been selected, the mood itself must next be attained.

The faculties of the attention must now be gathered up by a simple, direct, effortless technique. Under no conditions should the mind be made blank. Nor should the disciple wait hopefully for thoughts to think themselves. It is too soon for the Law to flow in with the forms. The artist must first paint his picture of the Law.

Choose an appropriate symbol. This symbol will be your mandala, and in most cases its cultivation will require considerable time. Do not be discouraged if it takes many months to clarify this symbol. Do not change

CHINESE WOODCUT OF THE BUDDHA REVEALING THE DOCTRINE OF ENLIGHTENMENT

symbols frequently, and never give up one design for another until the Law has been found.

The symbol may be an object, an ideal, or a pattern, but it must be capable of some definition; that is, it must be perceptible to the mind if not to the senses themselves. Abstract virtues like goodness, kindness, or unselfishness are not suitable in themselves as concentration symbols. It is for this reason that in the Eastern schools all of the virtues are pictured. Buddhism is personified by the Buddha, itself a personification of all of the abstract virtues of the doctrine. In Christianity the perfection of Christian virtue is figured forth in the life, sacrifice, and death of Jesus the Christ.

The teacher is not the Law, but bears witness of the Law. In concentration the disciple cannot concentrate directly upon the Law, but upon some pattern or imagery which bears witness. And he must never confuse the image with that which is imaged!

Frequently it is advisable to derive the concentration pattern from some phase of life which is pictorially meaningful. It has been pointed out that men often find Truth according to the inclination of their tastes. To the scholar his books are sacred. To the artist the laws and canons of art represent his natural approach to the discovery of the Law. The developed mathematician finds God in numbers, and the astronomer finds Truth in the stars.

Choose, therefore, as the first pattern for concentration some form or device which has already proved to be an inspiration and has brought you some measure of realization. Thus through the gateway of the known you pass naturally and normally into the presence of the Knower.

There is no broad restriction imposed on the selection of the proper subject. If you have found merit in it, or have gained merit through it, it is proper.

For the sake of an example, let us suppose that we are nature lovers. We have found inspiration and strength in contact with growing things. We have found the law in growth. We cannot concentrate upon the abstract principle of growth. Therefore let us select some one growing thing as the symbol of growth, always bearing in mind that we are not limiting growth itself but merely specializing it, so that it will remain within the boundaries of human comprehension. In this way we shall escape vagary and indefinition, abstractions which in turn would lead only to involvements and platitudes.

Of the growing things a tree is one of the noblest and most complicated of all forms in the plant kingdom, and at the same time the most symbolical. The tree from time immemorial has been used as a basis for diagramming many forms of human knowledge. In old prints and manuscripts we find trees of law, trees of medicine, and trees of religion. Races frequently are represented in the form of a tree and its branches. Several of the old philosophies have represented the entire universe in the form of a tree. Reflections upon a matter such as this is a proper prologue to concentration. It posits the realization of magnitude, and reminds the intellect of the universality of the selected symbol.

It is enough that a suitably symbolic subject be decided upon preparatory to the study of the following chapter, which continues the discussion of concentration.

FIFTH REALIZATION

The entire subject matter of this chapter is realization with the keynote: PIERCE THE FORM. Learn to recognize all ideas as essentially formless, but perceptible inwardly as manifestations of the Law.

When you read books, when you listen to teachings, when you contemplate the old wisdom, pierce the form. Ponder the words of Maimonides: "Beneath the body of the Law is the soul of the Law; and beneath the soul of the Law is the spirit of the Law." Search for the spirit of the doctrine. Accept nothing less.

In everything which occurs to you as incident or circumstance, recognize symbols of the formless. Realize that all visible physical bodies and all tangible, conceivable forms of knowledge are indeed the many-colored fringe on the robes of the Infinite.

Remember the inscription on the temple of Sais in Egypt: "I, Isis, am all that has been, that is or shall be; no mortal man hath ever me unveiled." Recognize the world as the veil, and realize that he who is entering into the hidden place must rend the veil of the temple from the top to the bottom. With the sword of insight, PIERCE THE VEIL AND FIND THE LAW.

VI

PHILOSOPHICAL ATTENTION

AN Eastern fable explains part of the mystery of concentration. It conveys certain implications that cannot be expressed in direct words. All spiritual values must be realized, inwardly comprehended—they cannot be communicated as mathematical formulas can be passed from one person to another.

The emperor of an Eastern country built a palace which he called the House of the Singing Floors. When the palace was finished he desired that gardens be planted about it so that the palace itself should stand in the midst of an earthly paradise.

The emperor sent for the wisest and most skilled of his gardeners and commanded him to landscape the palace grounds. The gardener, who was very old and very wise, went out from the palace, and selecting a place nearby built himself a crude sort of chair with a canopy of branches as a protection from the elements. The old man then seated himself there quietly. Summer slowly passed and the man sat silently watching. Autumn came; the leaves of the trees changed their colors and fell; the birds departed. The clouds gathered, and at last the snows of winter lay upon the ground. Still the aged gardener sat and watched. The winds whirled the snow, banking it up against the rocks. The trees bent under the fury of the gale. But the gardener merely drew his woolen cloak about him and reached for another steaming bowl of tea. Then springtime came. The snows melted; the little streams were filled; the squirrels came out from their holes; the spring flowers sent their green leaves through the patches of earth and melting snow. The gardener sat watching the motions of the seasons.

At last the summer came again. Having remained for a full year sitting in his chair of tree branches, the gardener rose, entered the presence of the emperor, and announced that now he would plant the garden.

A year later the earthly paradise was completed. Rare plants flowered on every hand. Curious fishes swam in the streams. Exotic birds nested in the trees. Little shrines stood upon the rocks, old stone lanterns bordered the pathways. In all the world there never had been so perfect a garden.

When it was all in readiness the gardener led the emperor out onto the broad porch of the palace and said to him: "O Son of Heaven, my work is finished. In every season and with the passing of every year this garden will retain its perfection. As each plant grows it will become a living part of a balanced completeness. When the leaves fall, they will form patterns upon the ground. And within the openings in the branches you will see the snow-capped mountains. When the streams rise, they will form pools and eddies, each of which will become perfectly patterned with the rest. It is for this reason that I sat in meditation for a year. There can be no conflict here. Each passing season will express its own beauty, in winter, in summer, in autumn, and in spring. There will be always harmonious beauty.

"As your majesty advances in years, your tastes will change, but the gardens will grow also. As long as you live you will find happiness in them. And when at last you return to the sky from whence you came, those who follow after you will find themselves in this garden as you have found yourself. I have built a miniature world that reflects the mysteries of a greater world. This, O Son of Heaven, is the wise man's garden."

To every man the fabled emperor is the *Self;* the garden, his life; and the aged gardener his wisdom with which he must build his earthly paradise. Wisdom opens the way and gives the example of concentration. The exercise and discipline of philosophical attention which we call concentration is exemplified in the gardener's year of meditation. Through the observation and consideration of all the universal processes which go on about us we become aware of the ever-changing seasons of the soul—summer changes to autumn, and autumn to winter, winter to spring, and spring to summer again.

This mystery of change cannot be understood by the reading of words, but it can be felt inwardly as a spiritual experience during concentration. Not only must we focus attention, but we must sense as eternal truth the gentle flowing of time through consciousness. We grow but in time toward eternity—gently, peacefully, inevitably. There must be no haste, no tension, no strain, and no striving. We must behold all things, value all things, feel our participation in all things; and from all these experiences find the garden of our living. When we do this year after year, life after life, we understand.

Tao, the way and the end in one, teaches that the method is forever flowing into the accomplishment; always the things we do are becoming part of the thing we are. To understand this *is* concentration; not merely the concentration of the mind with its tendency to scatter its resources, but more completely to understand our relationship with life so that the unity of our purpose is strong enough to bind all confusion together in one ever-flowing harmonious pattern.

CONCENTRATION AS A FORM OF EXPERIENCE

SOMETIMES it is difficult to understand that concentration is not essentially an intellectual process. While the mind is the instrument of concentration, the exercises fail if they are regarded as directed toward mental control through effort.

Also it seems hard to understand that concentration involves the simultaneous activity of every part of the consciousness. There must be attention without tension. There must be feeling without emotion; visualization without fixation. And all must be bound together by an inclusive one-pointedness of purpose which does not include any inference of limitation.

The process is more difficult to describe than it is to achieve, because it occurs simultaneously on different planes or levels. It depends for its success upon capacity to realize the identity of the parts of one's own consciousness; for example, that feeling and thought are one, and that the things sensed are identical with the power to sense. There is no division between the flower and its beauty, the bird and its grace, or the river and its song.

We may become aware of all values at the same time. This is properly termed spiritual perception. To the artist the tree is form; to the woodcutter it is fuel. The musician hears the rustle of its leaves. In it the mystic sees growth. To the pilgrim the tree is shelter; to the farmer its fruit is life; to the squirrel that lives in its hollow trunk it is protection; to the physician who makes medicine from its bark it is healing; to the carpenter it is walls and roof. The tree is all this and more to the sage in meditation beneath its branches. It is felt and known in all of its innumerable qualities and attributes. It is spiritual experience; it is Law; it is God; it is Truth. Concentration is the power or discipline by which all these values become simultaneously accessible as spiritual power.

Most of all, it is realization. Truth brings to the wise man exactly what the wise man brings to Truth. Therefore Truth is a sort of mystic fable, a living legend, which he interprets according to himself. Each finds in Truth what he himself is; according to his own knowledge he understands.

Through the practice of concentration the individual finds himself in all things and through all things. This is the reason why the old Masters of the Hidden Road, as they were called in Korea, often gave contradictory definitions. Concentration, they would explain to their disciples, was a mental process. Then, in the very next breath, they would insist that the mind had no part in it. The very contradiction was part of the fable, part of the mystery. It confused the foolish, enlightened the wise.

When Plato pointed to heaven as the abode of the gods, and Aristotle pointed to the earth as the abode of the gods, the confusion and contradiction seemed hopeless. Yet it takes but a moment of real understanding to know that both were right; that all differences are proof of unity. The materialist will scoff and declare such reasoning to be little better than madness. But to the wise the materialist is the maddest of all. Yet the sage and the materialist are both right. Realization will prove this, for realization is forever finding the right and abiding with it.

When you begin your practice of concentration, the rapidity of progress depends entirely upon the full understanding of what the discipline means. A bad start, that is, an effort inspired by inadequate comprehension, will result in years of comparatively fruitless striving. So there should not be too much haste or too much eagerness. Success depends upon thoroughness of understanding. It is for this reason that these pages reiterate in several ways the basic concepts. If the foundation is right, all that follows will flow in the proper course.

It may prove beneficial to consider your own personal proficiency in three basic capacities—your capacity to think in terms of spiritual realities; to feel in terms of impersonal participation in a universal sharing of life; and to visualize in terms of seeing values through forms.

This probably sounds rather confused, yet it is a common experience that the normal individual at this stage of universal growth usually has a greater capacity in one of these qualifications than in the other two. Some think better than they feel. Others react more correctly to visual stimuli. Try sincerely to strengthen whichever of these qualities seems the weakest in yourself. Your spiritual consciousnesss must be compounded from a balance of these three powers of your soul. The lack of one will unbalance the others and result in an imperfect approach.

It is also true that any tendency to introvert—the degree to which we cut ourselves off from the flow of life in others—damages our own sensitivity. All of the experiences of normal living contribute their part to our own soul power. If we restrict the flow of our own lives and narrow the sphere of our personal experience we frustrate the universality of ourselves. This is a common mistake among metaphysicians. There is no virtue in aloofness. We are not greater or more dignified because we separate ourselves from others. Our true greatness lies in the nobility of discovering ourselves in the dreams and hopes and labors of our world.

All of which means that the true concentration may be said to come about of itself. If we fulfill the Law in living, the Law sets up its own motion within our consciousness. We will then concentrate naturally as forms occur naturally. We will release soul power as the tree releases its buds and branches. Concentration is natural to man, but only when man himself is natural.

Concentration is the next step in the unfoldment of the inner self. Man cannot cause concentration, but he can prevent it. Unfoldment, therefore, is not the forcing of the exercise, but the removal of the obstacles to a perfectly natural and beautiful process in the consciousness itself.

If you can understand, you will do. Your action must flow from your understanding as from a fountain. At this point little can be added to the discipline. YOU must find the way. But if you will meditate earnestly upon what has been implied, you will not go astray. If the words are not yet sufficiently meaningful, you must understand that consciousness itself is not yet sufficiently free

THE CONTEMPLATION OF THE INNER IMAGE. THE DISCOVERY OF THE SELF IN THE SYMBOL OF THE NOT-SELF. THE REALIZATION OF THE BIRTH OF THE TRANSCENDENTAL BEING WITHIN. THE BEGINNING OF THE DISCIPLINE OF MEDITATION

from limitation of attitude and complexity to permit of proper concentration. Under such conditions you must continue the preparational disciplines. Do not be afraid to admit insufficiency, but rather accept insufficiency as a challenge from reality to yourself, and without disappointment or regret but with the deepest realization of universal wisdom set yourself to the task of fitting your consciousness and your life into the universal plan. When the time comes and you are ready, YOU WILL KNOW.

SPIRITUAL ALCHEMY

THE word alchemy is compounded from two words: *al* or *el* meaning God, and *Khem* meaning Egypt. Literally the word chemistry means the science of the Egyptians; alchemy the divine science of chemistry or the divine science of Egypt. Chemistry was identified with the Egyptians because among ancient peoples it was believed that the secrets of chemistry were first communicated to man by the priests of the Egyptian temples.

Alchemy is spiritual chemistry. It is the secret doctrine concerning the perfection of man, concealed under a terminology of chemical terms, allegories, fables, and symbols. Alchemy is an integral part of the European mystical tradition, and also occupies a position of similar importance in the Taoist metaphysics of China. Many of the greatest of the Taoist saints were celebrated for their proficiency in alchemical research and experimentation.

I have many times been asked why it was necessary or desirable to conceal spiritual truths in elaborate systems of fables and emblems. A student once asked me why it would not be much simpler and more helpful to leave all symbols behind and just explain the whole mystery at the beginning so that everyone could understand the facts themselves. By this time it is hoped that you have reached the point where you will understand why it is impossible to describe any spiritual reality except in terms of symbolism. No one can describe growth without recourse to a description of something that grows. Spiritual realities are internal formless mysteries, incomprehensible unless clothed in tangible lore.

The fable becomes the vehicle of communication. A man crossing the void between one mind and another must be transported in some kind of container. The Buddhists call their sacred scriptures ***baskets.*** When you have received the idea and made it a part of yourself, you then may discard the basket. One of the saddest tragedies of mankind is that the average human being saves the basket and throws away the contents; or mistaking the basket for the contents he worships the basket, believing he is pious because he preserves the shape of the idea that has come to him, even though he is unaware of the purpose.

Frequently my students have objected to the extremely fantastic nature of religious and philosophical symbolism and fable. This wild extravagance of fantasy is part of a well-planned purpose. It is a constant reminder that the symbols obviously are too extravagant for literal acceptance by the thoughtful; that they conceal principles which are beyond the sphere of our physical and so-called normal perception.

Take for example the alchemical symbolism of the unicorn. Out of fabulous antiquity has descended an account of a weird animal differing from any creature familiar to man. It was shaped like a horse, but had a cloven hoof. On its forehead grew a long slender horn of twisted gold. The tail of the unicorn was similar to that of a lion, and its mane was of spun silver. It lived alone in remote parts of the mountains, and there was but one alive at a time. It endured for many ages, and permitted itself to be seen at certain intervals. The unicorn of European mysticism is the *Ki-lin* of the Chinese, the lion-horse with the single horn, a fabled animal that announced the birth of Confucius. How does it happen that two races dwelling on opposite sides of the earth should share a belief in this mythological creature?

How beautifully the story of the unicorn fulfills the purpose of the ancient priests who devised it. Medieval zoologists frequently included the unicorn as an actually existing animal, assigning as its habitation some little-known and inaccessible place such as the Sahara Desert. The museums of Europe include in their collections several drinking goblets that belonged to feudal princes, which are reported to have been shaped from the horns of unicorns. Men wanted to believe that the fable was true; therefore to them it *was* true.

There was no mystery to the unicorn. It was merely a rare creature; one that found its way into the heraldry of many nations and families who bore the symbol but never sensed the meaning.

The modern world gave considerable debate to this fantastic creature. One modern school decided that the unicorn was a highly glorified rhinoceros; that the single horn peculiar to this animal had given rise to a strange story in the disordered minds of primitive people. Still, the symbolism was preserved. And the modern scientist was happy at having solved the mystery to his own satisfaction.

The alchemical book of Lambspring gives the key to the real meaning. The unicorn with its one golden horn, and living alone, is the human soul dwelling far distant in the impenetrable forest of the senses compounded from the numerous aspects of the *anima* itself.

This white horse with the horn is a proper symbol for the most profound meditation. There is no way to tell its story to the foolish, nor is there any way in which its mystery can be concealed from the thoughful. No man can describe the soul in direct and simple words. It is a subjective experience. But each man may restore for himself a certain pattern of the soul by meditating upon the appearance and temperament of this strangely docile animal, described by Basil Valentine as so shy that it runs before the hunter can reach it; so wise that it can never be captured in any net devised by man.

A symbol of the soul must likewise be a symbol of soul power. The golden horn, never used to injure any creature but around which the knight-errant tied the silken scarf, is the power of concentration, the one-pointedness of the soul, the harmless strength of Truth. But how could this be explained to men who would prize the unicorn's horn as a wine goblet? Whoever the initiated guildsman was who first fashioned that horn into a beaker, undoubtedly was acquainted with the mystery, for if there possibly could be devised a vessel to hold the mystic wine of the feast of Cana, it would be the unicorn's horn.

And so the mystery grows, each part fitting into the rest, each circumstance conveying an inference that literal words can only crucify and destroy. As the soul must be sought in the farthermost and the innermost intricacies of our lives, so Truth will be found hidden in the mystery of symbols. Symbolism is the old appointed way of telling the *Story*. The universe is the first symbol; man the most perfect symbol; and Truth the hidden reality behind all symbols.

THE CYCLE OF THE QUEST

THE alchemists belong to that group of mystics who are said to follow the "cycle of the quest"; that is, their symbolism is based upon a search for something lost or hidden. The Knights of the Round Table seeking the Holy Grail, the Illuminati seeking the Pearl of Great Price, and the alchemists seeking the threefold Elixir, all belong to the symbolism of pilgrimage. Truth is viewed as separated from man by a strange, intangible sense of distance; a space of time or place that must be crossed. But it is a distance of *becoming;* a search for that which is farthest from the known, but nearest to the Self. It is indeed a foolish mortal who mistakes spiritual distances for material intervals, or permits himself to dream of Reality in terms of place.

Alchemy is devoted to the quest of three hidden truths which are three concealments of one Truth. The first of the veils is the transmutation of metals; the second the discovery of a universal medicine; and the third the creation of the elixir of conscious immortality.

There were two kinds of alchemists. To the first, alchemy was a super-chemistry, the transmutation of metals a physical possibility, and the universal medicine an actual compound against disease, the elixir of life, a subtle fluid which could prolong physical existence indefinitely. To the second kind of alchemist the three quests were entirely spiritual, and were to be attained only through the practice of the mystical disciplines of realization that had descended from the ancient rites of the Egyptian temples.

In an old manuscript left behind by some unknown writer of the 17th Century, a mystic alchemist sounds the note of warning: "Woe! Woe! Woe unto the gold-makers!" This is the burden of all alchemical writings. The fables are told, but woe to him who accepts them as the substance of the doctrine. They are but the shadow; the substance lies beyond.

To the modern Truth seeker alchemy conveys the light of another facet of the philosophical diamond. It gives further instruction in the mystery of the search for the Self.

But first must come the mystery of the metals. There are two kinds of metals, the earthly metals and the philosophical metals. There is a kind of gold that is mined from the earth, and there is a philosophical gold that is mined from the air. There is a mercury which falls from the rock, and a philosophical mercury that abides as a vapor in space. There is mortal iron, and immortal iron. There is a tin in the earth, and a tin in the heavens; a copper that corrodes, and a copper that is incorruptible. There is a lead that is heavy, and a lead that has no weight at all.

In the formulas of alchemy there are seven sacred and profane metals, as in the formulas of theurgy there are seven parts of the soul, rational and irrational. The seven irrational parts of the soul are the seven base metals; the seven rational parts of the soul are the seven mysterious and perfect metals. Also there are seven sensory perceptions of the soul which extend outwardly from within to comprehend the order of the base metals, and there are seven rational extensions of the soul which extend inwardly to contemplate the divine metals.

In addition to the metals, there is *Vitriol;* not the vitriol of chemistry, but the Vitriol of the philosophers. It is the devourer of the metals; the slayer of the metallic souls. This Vitriol is the indispensable solvent of the metallic principles; it destroys them as metals and mingles their essences. It dies with them and produces from their minglings the supreme mystery of the philosophers' stone. This is the stone *petra;* the rock upon which must stand the temple of Truth. This is the stone that the builders rejected; the stone that destroyed the giant of Nebuchadnezzar's dream. This is the sling stone of David; the white stone; the magical stone of the Shedd that gave Solomon power over all the worlds. This is the emerald of the Sangrail, and the sapphire stone of the Commandments. This is the diamond soul of the Tibetan Lamas, the priceless jewel in the forehead of the Buddha.

Words can but imply the meaning, for in alchemy, as in Oriental mysticism, we are dealing with wordless principles and nameless facts. But dimly we may perceive or sense the majesty of the concept. Omar Khayyam knew the secret of the metals when he wrote:

> The Vine had struck a Fibre, which about
> If clings my Being—let the Sufi flout:
> Of my Base Metal may be filed a Key,
> That shall unlock the Door he howls without.

The mystery of the metals is the mystery of the recognition of the twofold nature of all consciousness, all form and all thought. When the alchemist wrote: "You shall take one part of the philosophical iron and add thereto three parts of the philosophical mercury, and be sure that they have been properly distilled and augmented," he was using his own quaint, picturesque terminology to convey a truly transcendental secret. Those searching for the mystery of the inner life can use in their quest only the higher and most attenuated faculties of sense and thought. The ordinary human mind is of very little service; the human emotions of very little good. We must seek within and find the spiritual powers of the mind, the spiritual powers of the heart, and the spiritual powers of the hand. In other words, we must use only the spirit of the metals.

It is useless to bring only the mortal perceptions and the mortal limitations to bear upon the problems of the immortal Self. Our physical experiences are not enough; they must be distilled and augmented. Our physical education is not enough; it is but a base shadow of something greater. Our thoughts, our sciences, our emotions, our arts, our actions, our crafts, are mortal and physical symbols of immortal powers. We must read all the symbols; we must seek all the shadows. This is the beginning of alchemy, that we shall discover our every word and deed to be but symbols, our hopes and aspirations only fables, our histories and traditions merely legends. All that we know, like the symbol of the unicorn, is an indication of that which lies within.

SIXTH REALIZATION

The almost inconceivable reality beyond all our experience and all our knowledge is an essential subject for our meditation. It must be a very sane and gentle meditation. It must not lead off into absurdities, but lead inward toward reality. Of all the fables in all

the world, we ourselves are the most fantastic. We are a creature stranger than any sphinx or chimera. The sphinx has the head of a man, the body of a lion, but what of man himself? He has the spirit of a god, the soul of a mortal, the body of an animal. He has dreams of space, the longings of the air, and the motions of the cosmos. Yet he is bound down like some Gulliver chained by Lilliputians. He is, of all creatures, the most mysterious, composite monster that dream ever fashioned.

In the ancient temple of Serapis at Alexandria stood a gigantic image of the weeping god. His body was fashioned out of the twigs and branches of trees; his hair was grass and grain; his eyes were precious stones; his garments were made of metal; and his body was overcloaked in the skins of animals. He was crowned with the feathers of birds; flowers bloomed in his hands; and insects gathered honey from his mantle. This weeping god upon whose head light shone down through the open roof of the temple, is man himself, the symbol of all nature, who bears within him all questions and all answers.

Thus we learn from the story of alchemy that each must gather the Elixir from all the lives that make up mankind, and compound therefrom the Elixir of his own life. From all the secrets that are man shall be fashioned the secret power that shall save man.

VII

THE ADEPTS

THE traditions of alchemy refer frequently to a mysterious order of adepts. It was believed of them that they possessed a complete knowledge of the mysterious elixir of life, could travel about the world appearing and disappearing at will, communicating their secrets to such as they deemed worthy.

These adepts carried with them the powder of projection, which they called the "Red Lion." A few grains of the "Red Lion" dropped upon a molten mass of crude metal would cause its instantaneous transmutation into the finest gold. According to one account the powder of projection could transmute one hundred thousand times its own weight. This same powder dissolved in wine was the philosophic elixir, the universal medicine against all corruptions of the flesh. According to von Welling, a minute particle of this "Red Lion" if placed on the surface of water would begin to revolve violently, passing through all the changes and periods which occur in the formation of a solar system.

In the majority of cases those alchemists who claimed to possess the powder of projection had received either the powder or the formula for its preparation from one of the nameless adepts. It is not, therefore, difficult to understand the veneration in which the invisible brothers were held. The great number of stories circulated describe the curious circumstances under which the adepts revealed their secrets.

Undoubtedly it is true that advanced alchemists possessing profound knowledge of the universal mystery did wander about medieval Europe, but the accounts of the adepts, like the story of the unicorn, were philosophic fables devised to deceive the unwary into holding false opinions regarding the alchemical operations.

The adept is the *Self,* the divine principle that manifests within the human personality, the reality behind every man. This Self possesses the true powder of projection, *wisdom*—for wisdom, and wisdom alone, can transmute all the base substances of human experience into spiritual power. The inward quest is the search for the Self. The purpose of concentration is to discover the Self. The end of all seeking after spiritual things is to be united with the divine part within. The conscious union resulting from the release of principle from personality, of the subtle from the gross, of the eternal from the temporal, is accomplished by means of the secret chemistry of the soul, the alchemy of the old world.

Within each of us is the adept Self, the rose diamond. On rare occasions we glimpse for an instant the tremendous implication of the Self, and we become aware that the personality is indeed merely a shadow of the real. These infrequent mystical experiences, these rare occasions when the sincere seeker feels himself to be in the presence of his own divine nature, were described in the old books as a visit from one of the adepts. In the extension of consciousness which resulted from such rare spiritual experiences came a newer, fuller appreciation of the mystery of the quest. The personality was instructed in sacred matters; it participated for an instant in a larger fact, and in this way came closer to the universal mystery of knowledge.

The laboratory is life. The alchemist is the Truth seeker. The formulas by which he attempts to control the metals are his disciplines of concentration and contemplation. The adept-teacher is the oversoul, and the powder of projection is living wisdom which transmutes all substances and all natures into the imperishable Truth for which all the world is seeking.

RETROSPECTION

ONE of the best-known of all philosophical disciplines is the Pythagorean exercise of retrospection. It is recorded that the members of the famous school of Crotona practiced a daily retrospection according to a formula laid down by the great master himself.

Retrospection is the mental process of reliving in reverse order the incidents of the day. The purpose of retrospection is to discover the moral weight of action.

The average person passing through the experiences of daily living is only partly aware of the significance of passing events. Some of the most valuable lessons go unnoticed. Failure to heed and observe, failure to discriminate and place right emphasis, and most of all, failure to be thoughtful—all these shortcomings deprive the consciousness of the experience of action. The result is that much valuable time is wasted.

By means of retrospection we may live again the incidents which have occurred; we may view them impartially; we may read our own actions as from a book. It is possible to see in greater perspective the intimate relationship between cause and effect. Theoretically, at least, retrospection enriches life, resulting in a greater thoroughness in thinking and feeling.

More recently the discipline of retrospection has been interpreted as a form of vicarious atonement. The person performing the retrospection sets himself up as a sort of judge and jury over his own actions. Reviewing the incidents of the day, he attempts to rationalize each of them. Subjecting his thoughts and emotions to a series of mental rewards and punishments, he sincerely regrets the mistakes he has made, and with equal sincerity acknowledges and applauds his more commendable accomplishments. This technique is regarded as highly beneficial in neutralizing karma. Unfortunately, it does not appear that this form of retrospection was practiced by the Pythagoreans. So we have no rule of conduct laid down by the master in this particular.

The practice of retrospection offers certain advantages if properly understood. But like most esoteric exercises it has been gravely misunderstood by most of those who have attempted to use it.

It is the natural purpose of the universe to keep the attention of man focused directly upon that hypothetical division of time which we call *now*. It is written in the Scriptures, "Now is the accepted time." Present action is the focusing of all the accomplishments and propensities of consciousness upon the problem of the moment. The *now* eternally is drawing out of man his resourcefulness, his courage, his integrity, and his understanding.

What we call time is so illusional that many philosophers have come to the conclusion that of all the dimensions of time, only the *now* is real. Any exercises which lure the point of consciousness away from the *now* are dangerous to those who are not well-grounded in the disciplines of realization. He who lives in the future abides in a vagary of hope. He who lives in the past lives in the vagary of regret. Both hope and regret are inferior attitudes as compared to the active certainties of the *now*. A man working with a present problem is gaining much more of soul growth than can be achieved by dreaming of unborn tomorrows, or moping over dead yesterdays. When we become very wise so that we are untroubled by memories and are unmoved by repining, we then may find profit in the contemplation of our own misdeeds. Until such time as we have gained this philosophical equilibrium, too much retrospection is likely to prove harmful.

There is a certain fatalism about the past, and so little can be done to unmake or remake that which already has occurred. As we have done, we have done. We may desire heartily and sincerely to take back the hasty words we have spoken, but we have spoken them to the air and the winds have carried them far beyond our reach. We never can bring them back. The kindly deed we might have performed is useless now. The occasion came and went. Performed tomorrow, it will be useless. The opportunity for experience which was offered and which we overlooked has passed on to others. We cannot lure it back. All we can do is settle back in the midst of our realization of failure and disappointment, discouraged by the helplessness and hopelessness of our miserable state. This negative attitude robs us in a very subtle way of a certain vitality.

Realization is not a discipline of repentance. It is a positive statement of conviction. It flows along the impulse to do and to be, and it has little in common with vain regret. It is better for man to search for Truth than it is for him to wrestle with his errors.

Another problem that arises with the discipline of retrospection (as it now is popularly practiced) relates to the implications of self-correction. Going through the experiences of the day the disciple is supposed to administer his rewards and punishments according to the merits and demerits of action.

This implies that the student knows what he should have done, and also that he knows what he should not have done. A critical survey in many cases indicates that true knowledge of correct courses of action is beyond the capacity of most students. Therefore the judgments made during retrospection are opinions little better than the actions themselves.

For example, a certain sect or school may teach that a disciple should eat only a certain kind of food. Quite thoughtlessly on some occasion the disciple eats something that is not included in the list. Later in his retrospection he realizes the enormity of his offense, enters into the process of self-chastisement which involves deep repentance and devout assurance that his sin will not be repeated, and feels a tremendous sense of personal failure.

Yet the truth of the matter may be that the group or sect which forbade the eating of the certain food was entirely wrong in its original condemnation. The dietetic restriction was not based upon a solid philosophical foundation, but upon the personal tastes of the founder of the sect. Perhaps this gentleman did not like onions; therefore he forbade his disciples to eat them.

In just this way the whole retrospective process becomes a vicious circle of misunderstanding and wrong emphasis, simply because the disciple does not know what is right and does not know what is wrong. In the deeper systems of philosophy the old teachers would have said that until the disciple actually knows *what is right,* retrospection is impossible; and when the disciple does know what is right retrospection is unnecessary. There is little virtue in a discipline that leads only to an inferiority complex.

Retrospection arises in all instances where the element of forgiveness of sin is present in a religious system; where there is some compromise of basic integrity. If the human being believes that there is any escape from the consequences of action, the standard of living will be compromised. Thoughtfulness must come first, not afterwards. A little wisdom is more precious than an ocean of repentance. To do what is right first, is to be wise. And so it is the first duty of the Truth seeker to search for the right. Having performed an action according to the noblest standard of consciousness, there is no cause for regret. If a mistake has been made, universal law will reveal it through karma. There should be thoughtfulness but not over-emphasis upon the daily process of living.

Often there is conflict between the larger vision and the smaller vision. I know individuals who have been possessed by regret and remorse for the greater part of a lifetime. Such persons sing their vices, but never have found their virtues. All too often their self-condemnation is based upon hopelessly inadequate standards of integrity; they are blaming themselves for faults which either do not exist or which have been highly magnified by popular ignorance.

In advising the discipline of retrospection I recommend a specially modified form of the exercise. This would agree almost exactly with the original Pythagorean formula. Appoint a few moments at the close of the day, become silent, relax, and permit the incidents of the day to flow through you as a series of pictures. It is customary in retrospection to reverse the order of the images, moving backward from last occurrences toward the beginning of the day. This is done in order that the relationship of effect and cause may be rendered more obvious by observing effects first and then tracing the causes of those effects backward along the line of incidents.

If the retrospection can be performed without any personal involvement, without any sense that the incidents are occurring to ourselves, the retrospection becomes philosophically useful. We should see, not the weaknesses of ourselves, but the *strength of the Law.*

We should not see ourselves as poor mortal sinners forever wrestling with the hosts of evil like Jacob with the angel, but rather we should see Law molding us eternally into the shape and purpose of its own reality.

Instead of worrying about our own soul growth; instead of being possessed by the desperate delusion of growing; instead of longing after some Elysian field, we should become aware of the workings of an ever-flowing Law by which all finite natures are being impelled and propelled.

Law is real; we are not. Law is good; we are not. Law is immortal; we are not. This does not mean that we are worms of the dust; insignificant, unimportant things; beings to live in misery and despair. Rather it means forgetfulness of ourselves. It is turning the effects of attention away from self-condemnation toward the face of fact. We know as a physical truth that he who forgets himself is happy. We are reminded of the biblical statement that the man who saves his life shall lose it. This applies especially in the field of religion.

Throughout the whole world of belief men are trying through their doctrines and their dogmas to save themselves. Through prayer and fasting, through rituals and dogmas, with candles and pyxides, self-centered mortals are bending to the task of saving themselves. Through self-depreciation, through self-denial, with flagellation and austerity, with gifts and offerings, the rich and the poor, the humble and the great are seeking divine favor, always for the same reason, always inspired by the same fundamental motive—self-preservation.

The soul must be saved, and strangely enough the salvation of an immortal principle is made to depend upon the ill-founded opinions of a frail and mortal part, the human personality. Men meditate to save themselves; and they practice retrospection to save themselves. Always they are thinking of the self; always plotting and planning for the self.

The lay disciple, falling into one of these pitfalls of the *Way,* comes inevitably to the dual conclusion that not only is he worth saving but that he is in dire and constant danger of being lost. In this wild game of saving and losing, of being redeemed and then relapsing, the beauty and nobility of living toward Truth is totally ignored. And man, when poised precariously between salvation and damnation, is not in a condition which induces an especially philosophic mood.

It is the purpose of realization that consciousness shall flow away from the personality toward identification with Law and reality. Posit the real, not the unreal. This is not a platitude, but a great spiritual truth.

When Jesus and his disciples were walking along the country road and they came upon the carcass of a dead dog, the disciples with various exclamations of disgust turned from the sight of the body which had begun to rot. But Jesus rebuked them, saying: "Pearls are not whiter than its teeth."

This parable—which originated somewhere in northern Asia and traveled far to be incorporated in the Christian traditions—is a statement of realization. It is applicable to the daily life of each disciple. By it we should judge others, and by the same rule we should judge ourselves. This does not mean that we should continue to cultivate old faults, but rather that we should strive to cultivate universal virtues. We should not excuse our own mistakes, but rather we should see through them and realize that they bear witness to a failure of adjustment between personal and universal understanding. We should not try to correct faults one by one, but rather with single-pointedness search for the one realization and the one truth that in itself corrects all faults.

Retrospection is serviceable if through the aid of it we come closer to the One. But if we are not more aware of good because of the exercise, then the exercise is not good for us. Any discipline that makes us feel our own inferiority is as wrong as one which makes us feel our own superiority. Man is neither great nor small. He is a channel through which eternal principle is flowing. He may think he is great, and then he truly is small. He may think he is small, and then perhaps he is great. But knowing he is a witness to a greatness that is not his own, which abides forever in the innermost and the furthermost, he is a sage established in reality.

If the retrospection appears to the consciousness as a practical method of growing, it may be practiced sparingly, but it should never become a crutch or an escape mechanism; should never be thought of as a compensation for action or inaction. If practiced at all, it should be keyed to the realization of works. Through observation and attention we should become more aware of the workings of universals through us and in us. If this is possible through retrospection, and the mind can protect itself from the processes so often associated with the discipline, then the effects can be beneficial.

Usually the discipline should be limited to from three to five minutes a day, and should be practiced regularly immediately before retiring. The mind should remain impassive and entirely calm. There should be no emotional reflex of any kind. It should be an experience in which we become aware, but to which we do not react as personal beings.

MORE ABOUT CONCENTRATION

ILLUSTRATING a preceding chapter is a figure representing the creation of the transcendental personality within the consciousness of one who is concentrating. We turn now to consideration of the next illustration of the same series, showing the extension or multiplication of the personality into three transcendent attributes. These figures require understanding and thought.

It is customary in Eastern theories of metaphysics to represent the heart as a shrine. Often this shrine is shown as a small Buddha-like structure within the breast. In some systems, especially the Buddhistic, the heart is described as a lotus bud. When this bud opens under the

THE THREE TRANSCENDENT ATTRIBUTES. THE REALIZATION OF THE THREE STATES OF THE SELF. THE HIGEST, OR SUPREME, STATE IS THAT OF ADI-BUDDHA, THE UNMOVED MOVER OF THE WORLD. THE BEOND, OR INTERMEDIATE, STATE IS AVALOKITESVARA, THE REALIZATION OF THE ONE, THE COMPREHENDER. THE SMALLEST FIGURE IS THE TERRESTRIAL BUDDHA, THE OBSERVER, THE BEHOLDER OF THE UNREAL, THE OBJECTIVE PERSONALITY WITH ITS ATTRIBUTES

gentle influence of the concentration, the seated figure of the meditating Buddha is found within. The heart is indeed a "House of Hidden Places," the very sanctuary of the body, the symbol of the throne of majesty in man. It is proper, therefore, that this, of all the organs in the bodily economy, should represent the Self, the reality, the most sacred part of the whole nature of the universe and of man.

The purpose of concentration is to become aware of reality. When this awareness is achieved it is described as coming to the one who discovers it and taking up its abode in his heart. Actually this is part of a symbolic story, but it conveys the idea.

In China, the oversoul or the reality sometimes is depicted as riding on the phœnix. It appears in the heavens and flies rapidly from cloud to cloud. At last, gliding downward, it disappears into the body of the disciple where it sits upon the lotus throne in his heart. When this mystery takes place a certain contact has been established; a bond has been forged between the personality and universal values.

This reality within is called the transcendent being. It is man's concept of the Universal Being. It is not the pure universal substance for the reason that the human consciousness is not capable of envisioning the Absoulte itself. The transcendent being is the Absolute *as we are able to understand it.* It is the infinite made finite by our own perception, yet incredible and unknowable to the concepts of the uninitiated and the uninformed.

To the degree that we are able to preserve and maintain the beauty, impersonality, and dignity of the transcendent being, to that degree we remain true to our philosophy and to our doctrine. As the mother carries her children within her body, so the disciple carries the transcendent being within his heart. It must grow up within him, ultimately to be born from him as a free and independent spirit. But the personality cannot survive the birth of the transcendent being. When the universal is born, the personal dies. It is written in the East that the mother of the Buddha lived but five days after the birth of her child.

The transcendent being is the *abiding presence.* Once it has been realized by concentration, it dwells with the disciple. This transcendent being never questions, never speaks, never demands. It merely remains—waiting. Understanding increases it; lack of understanding apparently causes it to diminish. But through this it gradually strengthens, becoming ever more dominant.

It is variously figured in Eastern mysticism. Quite often it is called the Maitreya, the bodhisattva which is to come. In this aspect it is the universal Messiah. This is the true import of the Messianic doctrine. The coming Savior is the transcendent being. In China, Maitreya sometimes is represented as a very rotund, smiling personality whose body seems to be perpetually shaking with laughter. It is a happy spirit abiding in man. There is nothing depressing or introverting about it. It is the joy of realization, the peace that Truth alone can bestow; a fortunate and desirable presence, the coming of which is to be marked by appropriate rejoicing.

The disciple having envisioned the real—that is, having become aware of his relationship to fact—is said to have attracted the transcendent being. From that time on the being grows with the rapidity of the evolution of the disciple. This is Jakob Boehme's tree of the soul which grows up in the heart until it fills the whole world. Gradually the transcendent being increases until man's personality becomes merely a dying atom in the substance of this universal reality.

Man begins his growth as a lowly creature like an atom in space. In the end, however, he achieves space; his consciousness is identified with space. He no longer is isolated, but encloses space within himself. In the Brahmanic books, Krishna is described as towering far above Arjuna, his faithful disciple. The transcendent being, Krishna, has in this manner so increased that in comparison to it the personality of the human creature is as nothing. The development of the transcendent being requires many lifetimes to consummate its final emancipation in a life of realization.

If I can convey in some way to you the meaning of the transcendent being, you will share one of the choicest secrets of Eastern esotericism. Here again we can make use of a fable.

Once upon a time there was an emperor who longed to have a son. Although he had many wives, Allah, in his infinite wisdom, gave him no sons. So the emperor resolved to go upon a pilgrimage to ask the advice and guidance of a great and noble saint who lived alone in the midst of a deep forest.

After many days of journeying, and numerous hardships and troubles, the king reached the hut of the hermit. Here he was nobly received by the holy Sufi. And to this aged and learned man the great prince of the earth told the sad story of his longings; of his desire that an heir might be born to him.

The Sufi listened to the sincerity of the king's appeal and said: "You shall have a son upon one condition."

"Anything that you ask," replied the emperor, "unto half of my kingdom. By Allah, whose name be praised, I swear it."

Within the year a son was born to the emperor. All his people gave thanks and the king was prepared to fufill his vow.

The holy Sufi came into his presence and the emperor said to him: "Ask what thou wilt."

The Sufi replied: "While I sit quietly in my hut in the deep forest, I wish you to remove the forest and to build in its place a great city so that without leaving the little garden around my house I may see the whole world go by and be among the concourse of peoples."

So the emperor built the city just as the holy man had desired. In the very midst of the city, protected by a beautiful marble dome, was the little hut of the holy man with its square of earth.

The holy man sat and watched the princes, the merchants, and the travelers from all over the world pass up and down before him. Several years had passed when he sent for the emperor. "I have seen enough," the saint observed firmly. "Remove the city."

So the emperor took all of his people and all of the merchants and their shops and the palaces and the gardens, and had them moved. What he could not move he deserted. And the holy man was alone again in the silence, surrounded by the ghosts of an empty city.

This is the legend of Fatehpur Sikri, the city of red stone and marble that today stands deserted. But it is more than a deserted city. It is the story of the transcendent being.

The emperor is the Truth seeker. The son he desires is his own immortality, continuance of himself as a spiritual truth. The holy man is the secret doctrine; the wisdom which finally becomes personified as the transcendent being.

The pilgrimage to the holy man's hut in the forest is the practice of the disciplines. The city that the emperor builds represents the cycle of incarnations in which the pagentry of lives takes place. The concourse of people who pass to and fro before the holy man's hut represents the various personalities that comprise the cycle of incarnations.

The holy man's hut around which has been built the temple with its marble dome is the abode of the transcendent being seated in the heart of the city, spectator to all that occurs. The transcendent being demands after the passing of many years that the city be moved and deserted, so that it may be left to sit alone in peaceful contemplation—the transcendent being having come into complete rulership over the life.

Finally nothing remains but the transcendent being; a creature built from the noblest hopes and aspirations, which is the real Self; the ego of the personality is dissolved in a universal essence. Man no longer lives for himself or by himself. He exists to fulfill the impulses of the transcendent being. He lives to bear witness to the will and purpose of the universal spirit that has taken up its abode within him.

Through contemplation and concentration it is possible to realize the transcendent being as very real and entirely substantial. It is a substance akin to the substance of a fact, shrined within the holy of holies of man's temple. The transcendent being becomes purposeful living, and the objective personality becomes its willing and obedient servant.

"I bow before the lotus throne," chants the enraptured Buddhist.

He means just that. As a personal creature he bows before the lotus throne of his own heart where sits Sakyamuni, the light of Asia and of the world, the priceless jewel, the transcendent being.

SEVENTH REALIZATION

To feel oneself or to realize oneself as the keeper of a sacred trust is a great experience in consciousness. In some way it adds to one's dignity, at the same time keeping one very gentle and humble. It is thus that each becomes his own high priest; his heart the altar; the transcendent being the god that dwells in the holy place. Religion becomes an intensely intimate and personal matter when the transcendent being is the direct object of all religious observance.

It is the god which abides with man. It is not a god but a ray of the God, the Principle, the Truth. It mingles through a mysterious alchemy with the mortal parts of man, though it is never limited or destroyed by them.

It stands, has stood, and shall stand. It remains the silent watcher. It is not the voice of conscience for it never criticizes, never blames, never doubts, never questions.

Like the passionless face of the meditating Buddha it sits in the heart and waits; waits through the ages during hundreds of lives, unmoved and unchanged, with ever-closed eyes and imperturbable, passive features. It waits for the day of liberation. There is no hurry, for there is no time. There is no delay. There is only a timeless

mystery waiting for liberation—waiting and yet not waiting, for here waiting has no reference to time. Timeless waiting is a mystery that is all wound up in realization; in the sublime secret of personal awareness.

Of all the mysteries of Asiatic metaphysics none is more sublime in its concept than the doctrine of the transcendent being, the ever-coming Self. While man builds his own soul he really is building the universal soul with virtues not his own; he is building virtues with wisdom that rises not in himself; and he is perfecting a wisdom apart from himself.

All the constructive and creative powers which man expresses fall into his personality from some deep and hidden source. Their purpose is not to build his personality, but to perfect the transcendental being which, born in the manger, a symbol of its material environment, unfolds and develops until it becomes a world savior, truly the savior of each man's world.

VIII

EXTENSION OF CONSCIOUSNESS

IN the Taoist system of philosophy the genii, that is, the intermediary spirits, frequently are depicted as riding through the air on strange, brightly plumaged birds. Such pictures convey a profound philosophic meaning and are part of the meditation symbolism.

In the old Mysteries genii represent the intellectual extensions of the personality. For example, in the course of numerous rebirths the Self or Oversoul gathers the harvest of experiences. Each life with its sequence of incidents enriches some part of the composite spiritual nature. In one incarnation the emphasis may be upon observation, whereas another life may be confronted especially with problems of discrimination. When the sattva or Self emanates a new composite personality at the beginning of each physical incarnation, that personality is composed of the substances of previous experiences. Thus the personality may be regarded either as a single entity or as a compound made up of numerous separate and distinct experience sequences. When considered as a single entity the incarnating ego is called the personality; but when considered as a composite structure it is made up of numerous separate experience cycles which have been named the genii.

These diverse experience principles riding on the brilliant plumage of the thought-bird soar about through space, flying up and down the world, each living out its smaller cycle within the larger cycle of the complete life. The genii are usually depicted as grotesque little creatures somewhat human in appearance huddled up in voluminous cloaks and robes, carrying or accompanied by the particular symbols of the qualities which they represent. The genii convey to the Eastern mind, by the manner in which they are drawn, a definite airy or unearthly quality. Their robes flow about them in whorls of color. They ride amidst the clouds. Frequently there is a humorous, mischievous look on their faces, and nearly always they convey the impression of traveling with great haste toward some strange, undefined destination.

The genii may be likened to vagrant thoughts. We sit down quietly to think about some serious or weighty concern. Suddenly, in the midst of our contemplation, our thoughts fly off to some entirely irrelevant subject. Then we must gather up our minds and start again. And even as our mental fingers reach out to catch the flying sprites they slip away again with mocking smiles. As the Chinese poet said, "The thoughts of men are ever escaping from the bondage of the will, longing to return to the sky."

There is considerable difference of opinion as to the proper method of coping with the complex phenomena of the personality. It has been usual in the Western systems of philosophy to attempt to point the mental processes into a single power administered by the dictatorship of the will. All of the faculties of the intellect must become one-pointed and one-purposed, having no freedom of their own. The result is a constant struggle in the self to reconcile the contradictions which arise among the senses and perceptions. The Oriental mystic does not favor this technique of development. Rather he prefers to permit the consciousness to flow outward along the magic airways of the mind.

In the imperial collection of paintings on exhibition in Peking is one which illustrates the Oriental viewpoint. In the background of the painting is a dim blue haze of distant mountains symbolizing the unknown elements toward which all life is ever seeking to escape. In the foreground is a thought genie seated astride a heron. beside the genie, holding onto the flowing robes of the little spirit, is the figure of a philosopher riding off to the mountains. The whole painting is one of joy and adventure—the reason is flying away on the wings of its own fancies.

To examine the subject more critically is to explore into one of the deepest mysteries of the contemplative life. Philosophically, the personality is not one being, one entity, one principle, or one force. Each new personality that comes into birth is a gathering up of other lives of distant times and of diversified impulses. As the woodchopper comes home with the bundle of faggots on his back, so the body brings into birth a bundle of twigs which it has gathered through innumerable incarnations.

One of the great experiences of living is adjusting to the fact of internal diversity. Looking about him, man realizes that he is personally confronted with problems of adjustment. He must learn to mingle with the multitude of other human beings who make up his world. He must adjust to numerous temperaments, and he must develop patience, sympathy, understanding, and all those qualities by which contact with others becomes just and harmonious.

Turning inwardly to contemplate the subtle mystery of himself, he again finds himself in the presence of diversity. His inner nature is not one, but many. If it were not so there would be no richness to living. It is the manyness within himself which makes it possible for him to mingle constructively and reasonably with the manyness that makes up his outer world. Within each of us is a universality, and this universality makes it possible for us to sense or to be aware of the universality of Space. The parts of man's consciousness bear witness to the parts of world consciousness.

The egocentric philosopher dreams of the time when he shall be all-knowing. He is conceited enough to believe that from his mortality may be fashioned a vessel which can contain all the knowledge of the world. He always is trying to find Truth within himself and to bind it there. But he has not yet advanced into the mystery of finding himself within Truth. As surely as all of the laws and truths of life are represented within man, so man himself is part of all the laws and principles of life wherever they may be and however they may be manifesting.

This brings us to a consideration of the extension of the personality along the lines of conscious impulse.

THE MYSTERY OF THE TRANSCENDENT PERSONALITY

THE transcendent personality is related to spiritual alchemy. Paracelsus, among others, refers to the mystery of the creation of artificial human beings. Such creatures were called *homunculi,* and usually are described as crystal-like in appearance and as produced by art rather than by nature. Art is always to be understood as philosophical discipline, as contrasted to nature which more slowly accomplishes the same ends by the gradual process of evolution. The homunculi were said to be born within eggs of glass. Their food was the universal medicine. They might not be shown to anyone who was not initiated, and they continued to exist as long as they received proper nourishment. They grew like human beings, but never became old. Although the homunculus is often referred to in alchemical writings, no tract containing any complete discussion of the subject is known to exist. As a result this entire cycle of symbolism and the meaning which it conceals has for the most part been ignored.

It is extremely difficult to explain the subtle process taking place within the unfolding consciousness of the developing mystic. It is evident that as realization increases the personality undergoes definite change and modification. Through growth each becomes a new or different person, yet the old personality is still present. Nothing is lost, but something is added. This new something is an intangible personality made up of understanding, appreciation, realization, and many other attributes of soul power. If the disciple progresses normally in his unfoldment, this new and transcendent personality becomes his true self, more real, more tangible than the temperament and character with which he was born.

Most important of all, this transcendent personality has a freedom about it, a space-quality. It is not limited by the habits, attitudes, tendencies, and characteristics which afflict and limit the mortal personality. This is the secret of the second birth. The transcendent personality is born within the consciousness of the mortal personality and grows up within the mind and body until it reaches a

THE EMERGENCE OF THE TRANSCENDENT PERSONALITY DURING THE PRACTICE OF REALIZATION. THE VEHICLE OF FREE CONSCIOUSNESS IS DEPICTED AS ESCAPING THROUGH THE PARIETAL FORAMINA, CONNECTED TO THE BODY BY A CLOUD OF MAGNETIC VAPOR condition wherein it is capable of independent existence. Having achieved its maturity, the transcendent personality, though still connected with the nature which is the source of itself, becomes capable of independent existence and may go and come as it pleases through the numberless gateways of consciousness.

For the transcendent personality all walls are doors, and the whole world is a gate. This is the secret of Zen which reveals how differently the East and the West view the mystery of life. The Occidental, seeking for salvation, has been taught that the gate which leads to eternal life is small and narrow; difficult to find. The Zen priest believes that the gate which leads to eternal life is so broad that it is no gate at all. It is everywhere. All life is forever flowing through it. It is the "gateless gate." Man cannot find it because he cannot realize that Space itself is the doorway to eternity. He is looking for a small door through life, when life itself is the doorway. The transcendent personality goes and comes through the "gateless gate," gradually revealing through the life he lives, the life that is living him.

For the purposes of meditation and realization you should now attempt the gentle contemplation of the structure of the Transcendent Being. Realize in terms of freedom. Think not of life that is limited by state or estate, but rather of life lived in Space. It may not be possible for you to travel physically to all parts of the world, or to read all of the books in the world, or to master all of the arts and sciences of the world in one lifetime, or even in many lifetimes. Yet we can always and forever move freely to and fro across the world. We may abide with all learning; we may sense through appreciation all of the learned accomplishments of man.

Otherwise stated, we may abide eternally in the presence of the Desire. This likewise is the mystery of the Sufi—the Persian mystic who, seated quietly in meditation, transfers his consciousness from his mortal personality to his transcendent personality, and by this means releases himself into the greater sphere of the mystic world.

MOTIVE

NOW comes a very vital and important consideration—motive. If man seeks release for motives of escape, he fails utterly. The rose garden of Sadi is not for those who are merely tired and weary and discouraged; rebels against the four walls of their little rooms. *The rose garden is for the one who loves the roses.* It is fulfillment and not escape. It is opportunity, not evasion. The transcendental sphere is not for those who would run away from living, but for those who would hasten forth toward life.

It is hard to describe the difference in motives, but once they are experienced the differences are obvious. The element of ulterior motive is involved; that certain deceit about many of our impulses which are inspired by a phase of selfishness, or self-pity, or egotism, or even ambition.

A textbook on the art of Chinese poetry explains the matter very simply. Three manners of men attempt to write poetry. (In Taoism, poetry is a symbol of harmonious or rhythmic living.) The first and lowest of these composes rhymes to sell, and his motive is profit. He can never become a true poet.

The second composes his lyrics to impress others with his superior abilities, or in the hope that they will advance him in reputation or preferment. His motives are egotism and ambition, and he can never be a poet.

The third class—and their number is comparatively small—are impelled only by the universal impulse of beauty. Poetry writes itself through them. Desiring neither profit nor fame, but moved by an irresistible impulse to express poetry, they alone are the poets. They have no personal motive, but a universal motive possesses them. It is the joy of beauty to reveal itself.

Likewise, it is the joy of the transcendent personality merely to be. It moves back and forth through the world like a spinning shuttle, drawn where beauty and nobility abide; rejoicing in the contemplation of that which is noble and good. In the words of Jami, "It is enough to be close to the beloved." The transcendent personality finds the beloved in Space.

The realization of these mysteries brings with it a very gentle mood, one still and peaceful, not sad or solemn. There is nothing grave or somber about the real. It is just that in the presence of true joy, as in the presence of deep sorrow, the Self is silent. Only that which feels little and lives superficially reacts boisterously.

In your meditation, if you have understood correctly, you may meet your own transcendent personality as one you have long known. You will discover a very simple, gentle creature, slightly humorous, very human, childlike in simplicity, but old as the world in wisdom. As you open the gates which lead outward into the spheres of your realization. this transcendent personality, bearing yourself with it, will move out through all the gateways, exploring, examining, experiencing, enjoying. Most of all, you will be with it in everything that it does. You will share its experiences. As time goes on you will realize that this transcendent personality is actually yourself. All that it does you will do. As you have builded it, so now it builds you into itself.

The transcendent personality is symbolized in Christian mysticism. It is truly the "Christ in you, the hope of glory." Its creation in you is the Second Advent. And its coming of age within your consciousness is the true "Christening."

In one of the apocalyptic Gospels there is the story of the child Jesus and the birds. While playing, Jesus fashioned pigeons of clay and tossed them into the air. As he did so they came to life and flew away into the sky. The transcenden personality is the magician of old; the Merlin of innumerable myths and legends. It possesses the magical power of bestowing life. It is the creator, the controller, the master of the *genii*. It is this transcendent being which releases the thought-spirits that fly about it. Omar Khayyam pictures them as "shadow shapes that come and go."

THE FABLE OF THE BIRDS

IN ancient times there lived in China a great and powerful emperor who richly patronized the arts and crafts. He surrounded himself with painters, sculptors, and ingenious artisans who competed with each other to provide the emperor with extraordinary examples of their talents and skill. One of these craftsmen built a golden cage so intricate in its design and so perfect in its workmanship that the equal of it could not be found among all the treasures of the earth. The cage was fashioned in the likeness of a temple, its many roofs encrusted with jewels and its interior divided into numerous rooms with mechanical doors and gates.

So delighted was the Son of Heaven at receiving this remarkable treasure that he immediately bestowed upon its designer the jade button and made him a prince of the empire. The emperor then called together his hunters and fowlers and bade them go forth with their nets to capture for him the strangest and most beautiful birds in the world.

After many adventures which rivaled the strange tales in the *Arabian Nights,* the fowlers returned and presented themselves before the emperor. Each in turn recounted his exploits and presented the rare birds he had captured. At last the chief of those who had gone forth brought as his offering the phœnix bird itself, which he had captured on the mountain of the moon.

The emperor set up his golden cage in the palace garden, and in each of its rooms he placed one of the rare birds. He then ordered the throne to be brought out, and seating himself he spent many hours contemplating the beautiful spectacle.

While he was seated thus, surrounded by his mandarins and princes, a Taoist monk knocked at the palace gates. There was a mystery about this monk. He did not walk down the road; he came from the sky in a cloud. He was a spirit. Entering into the presence of the emperor the monk seated himself with dignity, and inquired about the golden cage. The emperor explained what had occurred.

The old man sadly shook his head and discoursed in this manner: "O Great Majesty, set not this example for your people. Release the birds and destroy the cage."

The emperor was displeased and astonished. He ordered the sage to explain himself.

The monk then continued: "You, O Son of Heaven, are the symbol of righteousness to all that live within your domain. You are the model man. Your actions are the laws of your empire. Your conduct is the rule for right and wrong. Great is your responsibility because all must look to you as to the source of common good.

"This cage, built in the form of a temple, is a threefold mystery. First of all, it is the world with its many rooms within which all life is imprisoned. In the second place this cage is China, the middle kingdom of the world. And you, O Emperor, and all your glittering court, are the imprisoned birds. Their bright plumes are your robes of state. And the phœnix is your very self. Your palaces are prisons; your temples are cages; your powers are nets which catch yourself. In the third place, this golden cage is your mortal nature. And these little feathered things are the dreams and hopes which are imprisoned within the very bondage of yourself. All that you have learned of poetry and music and art; all the beauties which you have come to understand and appreciate and comprehend, are held prisoners within the cage of your mortal consciousness.

"O Emperor, release them all, and in releasing them, release yourself. Hold nothing captive. If you keep these birds in their gilded cage they will cease to sing. Each in turn will pine away and die. It was not the purpose of life that it should be imprisoned or bound, and the one who keeps these birds in the cage will destroy them, and in the end destroy himself.

"You have found joy in capturing the birds. Now find the greater joy, the truly imperial privilege of releasing them."

As he finished speaking, the old monk drew his robes about himself and disappeared in the very presence of the emperor. The emperor, himself a scholar, realized that the being who had appeared in the robes of the monk was no ordinary mortal but a celestial creature, the heavenly guardian of the birds. And as heaven had directed, so the Son of Heaven obeyed. He ordered all of the cage doors to be opened so that the imprisoned birds might fly back to the sky. Then he took the cage to the mountains and left it with all of the doors open, setting aside the place as a sanctuary for the birds.

As the years passed many of the birds returned to the cage and built their nests in it. And when the emperor was tired with problems of state he would go out and climb the mountains to stand for hours watching the birds that flew in and out through the open doors of the cage. At the end of his life he wrote a poem describing the understanding that had come to him from the contemplation of this mystery.

The story explains itself, yet it tells much more than might first be understood. We live in a world which each of us in his own way has the impulse to dominate. We desire to capture life within the nets of will and thought. We measure success in terms of dominion. We feel that we are great in the measure that we possess. These reactions and impulses are entirely contrary to the contemplative life. Yet the attitudes involved are so subtle and insidious in their operation that we learn our mistakes only after lifetimes of error.

The difficulty with so-called spiritual ambition is the limitation which it inevitably imposes upon the free motion of life. As a concrete illustration: Assume that all honest and sincere persons desire Truth. Each in his own way seeks to capture the Real, yet each seeker consciously or unconsciously thwarts his own ends. He does this by imposing the limitations of his own ignorance upon the very Reality which he seeks to discover.

Student Number One destroys Truth by declaring that one must practice yoga to discover it. Student Number Two destroys Truth by affirming that he can discover the Real through the intensive study of chemistry. Student Number Three destroys Truth by taking mathematics as the key to universal knowledge. Student Number Four destroys Truth by maintaining that it can be discovered by the practice of austerities. Student Number Five destroys Truth by insisting that Reality can be achieved through pilgrimage. Student Number Six destroys Truth by declaring that understanding can be won through contact with holy relics. Student Number Seven destroys Truth by maintaining that it can be discovered in books. And Student Number Eight destroys Truth by denying that it can be discovered in books.

Each in his own way follows along the lines of his own endeavors and tries to capture eternity with the instruments of his own opinions, demanding that Truth be what he expects it to be. Unconsciously he sets himself up as a judge over the unknown, while in his ignorance he takes the attitude that could be reasonable only if he were all-knowing.

It does not follow that Reality is not to be achieved through meditation, or through study, or through mathematics, or through the practice of austerities. Each grows according to his own understanding. But as theology has corrupted religion, so formulas have corrupted philosophy.

The doctrine of the transcendent personality assumes that the quest for Reality is not a formularized attempt, but a spontaneous adventure in consciousness. There is no need for prodding the consciousness toward the quest for the Overself. Man's spiritual nature is not a lazy schoolboy who must be browbeaten into a state of learning. It is the impulse of the Self to flow toward the Real. There is no need to stimulate this impulse. All that is necessary is to remove the artificial impediments and obstacles set up by the chemistry of the physical personality.

As the bird flies from the cage when the door is opened because the bird belongs to the air, so consciousness flies to the Real when the cage of material limitation is opened.

TRANSCENDENTAL BEING

IN meditation the transcendent personality is first visualized as born in the aura of the heart. Here it remains seated in contemplation of the Law. As realization increases, the transcendent personality ascends along the course of the vagus nerve to the brain. Here it seats itself upon the thousand-petaled lotus—the aura of the pineal gland. As the disciple proceeds, his personal consciousness mingles with that of the transcendent personality, with the result that the center of awareness ascends likewise to the brain and mingles with the transcendent personality to form the *Transcendental Being*.

A simple example of this power of consciousness to localize or directionalize, is the mystery of pain. Pain is a process of becoming acutely aware of some one part of the body. Thus a pain in the hand causes one to become hand-conscious—the center of consciousness moves into the hand and creates an acute sensitivity. When the center of consciousness moves into the transcendent per-

THE SEVEN PRIMARY LAWS OR MOTIONS OF TAO ARE EMANATED AS MODES OF THE TRANSCENDENTAL BEING. REALIZATION ESTABLISHES THE FOUNDATIONS OR POLARITIES OF REALITY WITHIN ITSELF

sonality it ceases to activate the material sense perceptions, but hovers over them, nourished and sustained by their testimony.

In Taoist paintings the Transcendental Being, which is the union of the consciousness and its projected image, ascends through the crown of the head and is represented as standing or sitting upon a little cloud rising upon a thread of incense smoke. The door of the cage is now open. The Transcendental Being has escaped from the personality complex.

Next arises the mystery of the multiplication of the Transcendental Being. Having established itself as a center or pole of consciousness outside of the personality, the Transcendental Being casts off the shadows or reflections of itself—six from the one, making the sacred septenary. The Transcendental Being thus becomes sevenfold in its manifestation, but remains unified in its essential substance. As planets are within the body of the sun, though cast from it, so the extensions of the Transcendental Being are part of its own essential unity although emanated by it. The six extensions assume their position as lords of the six directions of qualitative space The Transcendental Being itself remains as the center or axis of the wheel.

By their meditations the lords of the six directions create the hierarchies of further emanations. These are the *genii.* The whole pattern together is Ezekiel's wheel filled with winged creatures and many eyes. In the midst of this Mercavah or chariot rides the Transcendental Being.

When this mystery has been achieved in the consciousness through realization, the disciple is ready for his adventure with the Real. The Transcendental Being can move up and down through time, back and forth through space, moved by one of life's most beautiful impulses, pure and unconditioned appreciation.

EIGHTH REALIZATION

This realization is the magic of appreciation. We are enriched and vitalized, strengthened and ordained, by the baptism of appreciation. To appreciate, we must understand. To understand, we must know. To know we must seek. To seek, we must desire. To desire, we must experience. To experience, we must feel.

Thus step by step we move from the temporal to the eternal along a sequence of normal impulses. Attempt the experience of appreciation. Observe, ponder, and wonder a little at the exquisite integrity which is present in everything everywhere in life. To appreciate is to enrich the Self. Yet appreciation demands nothing but the right to be silent and a little humble in the presence of a great good or a great beauty.

IX

MATERIAL AND METAPHYSICAL PERSONALITY

THE material personality is composed of the sensory perceptions with their reflexes, the mind, the emotions, the imagination, the generative powers, and the physical body.

The metaphysical personality is an alchemical distillation of these faculties, forces, and members. Through the process of experience or evolution, all of the physical extensions of consciousness are being sublimated into transcendental energies. This is the philosophical explanation of the mystery of the *psyche* or soul.

The material personality consists of a number of parts co-ordinated into one functioning unit. The superphysical personality reflects this same diversity united or bound together by realization, in its aspect as *understanding.*

In the Tibetan symbolism the figure of the Buddha representing complete realization is frequently depicted as accompanied by two bodhisattvas. This triad symbolizes realization *per se,* and its principal conditions or aspects. The intellectual extension of realization is personified by the bodhisattva Manjusri, and the emotional extension of realization by the bodhisattva Avalokiteshvara.

Manjusri usually carries in one hand the flaming sword of detachment, and is accompanied by the peculiar symbol of the intellect, a book supported in the heart of a lotus blossom.

Avalokiteshvara, the Lord of Compassion, usually depicted as androgynous (uniting the characteristics of both sexes), is placed in a devotional posture, sometimes carrying an egg or pomegranate.

Manjusri, realization as mind, ponders the mystery of life. It represents the Self as the seeker, realization moving toward the thing to be realized. This bodhisattva, in the doctrines of Lamaism, is the lord of magic, astrology, oracles, incantations, and charms. It conjures up the worlds, and then with its flaming sword destroys the very phenomenal universe it has engendered.

Avalokiteshvara, or Kuan Yin, represents the Self as the thing sought. It is the realization of the identity of the Self and the object of its desire. It is therefore the Prince of Compassion, the service of the Self in all else that exists; the performance of right action, the conduct of man toward his own Self in other beings. The worship of Kuan Yin begins with the recognition of the omnipresence of the Real and ends in a mystical union with the Whole of life.

Manjusri is the sun and Avalokiteshvara is the moon in the esoteric symbolism. This does not mean the physical bodies of the planets, but the mystical powers for which these orbs stand as witnesses in Space. In Buddhist physics they are referred to as centrifugal and centripetal motion.

The intellect is centrifugal, or motion out from Self. Compassion is centripetal, or absorption into Self. Between these two is the supreme, immovable power of Truth, represented by Buddha itself, unchangeable in the midst of motion, the only force known to man in which all motion is held in suspension.

The superphysical personality is represented by this triad of Tibetan divinities. The sublimation of all intellectual impulses perfects the principle of mind; the sublimation of all emotional impulses perfects the principle of emotion. It is taught that the celestial bodhisattvas, the *heavenly Selves,* like the gold and silver of alchemy, are the distillations of their corresponding material impulses. As the tides ebb and flow, so realization moves outward and inward. The outward motion is along channels of thought, and the inward motion is along channels of feeling. This is the soul-breath, the control of which is one of the deepest secrets of yoga.

The student must learn to apply these truths to the problems of his daily living. He cannot accomplish in a few years, or even in a single lifetime, all that is implied. But it is possible through right action and right aspiration to live toward the All. So if we remain firm and devoted in our allegiance to Truth, and proceed according to right understanding, our growth will be continuous even though actual progress may appear woefully slow.

The centrifugal motion of the intellect manifests materially as the urge to know. This impulse is fulfilled or satisfied through the accumulation of knowledge on four levels or planes. In the East these levels are termed directions or corners, and are under the rulership of the *lokapalas* or kings of the hollow square. Each lokapala is the ruler over a sphere of essential learning, and in Oriental symbolical art all are accompanied by proper symbols of their qualities. These kings represent also the laws governing the four planes of intellectual manifestation.

In the universe each world has its own laws. To master a world or sphere means to adjust oneself perfectly to the law of that sphere, at the same time retaining immovable identiy. The four *lokas* or regions of the lokapalas are the sacerdotal sphere, the administrative sphere, the economic sphere, and the sphere of crafts and trades.

The *sacerdotal sphere* includes religion, science, the arts, languages, the learned professions, literature, magic, and philosophy.

The *administrative sphere* pertains to leadership, the struggle for physical establishment in a world of competitive ambitions and all that pertains to the right use of possessions, impulses, emotions, attitudes, and the imaginative power.

The *economic sphere* corresponds to the industrial estate of the modern world. It is the world of barter and exchange, of buying and selling. More profoundly, it is perception of the responsibilities of the social order, man's place in a world which can sustain him only if he shares with others in the common responsibilities and opportunities of living.

The *sphere of the crafts and trades* is that of physical labor. It involves the problem of production, and includes the agriculturalist, the craftsman, the mechanic, and all who labor with their hands in working the basic elements of material life.

Realization must extend through these four worlds, conquer them through adjustment, and participate in their activities, though never for a moment must man be held prisoner within the walls of the hollow square. Through the four gates guarded by their demon kings, realization must flow freely; the consciousness must be in the worlds but not of them. To lose the sense or realization that the Self is superior to its conditions is to fall into *Maya* or delusion. The Self is the lord of conditions, though it must experience condition and remain unconditioned.

To fail in this adjustment is to fall prey to the lokapalas. The moment that man through intellectual error loses perspective, and identifies himself with or assumes the reality of any of the four planes, the worlds become hells and experience changes into suffering, for suffering is experience without realization.

Emotion is part of the centrifugal experience of realization. Through the intellect, man discovers diversity. By discrimination he recognizes, at least intellectually, the one universal All and the one universal Self which is at the root of diversity. By compassion, which is the transmutation of passion, he draws diversity back to himself, or more correctly, he becomes great enough to enclose or include diversity in his working realization of unity. Here again the emotional nature operates through the mystical equivalents of the four *lokas* or worlds.

In the Eastern symbolism, the *lokas* or planes have their overtones which are called *talas.* It is usual to define a *loka* as a place, and the *tala* as a state or a condition; but these definitions must be understood philosophically. For example, intellectually the sacerdotal sphere is an area of experience to be mastered; emotionally it is a mood, a feeling, an attitude, which must be drawn back into the Self and included within the consciousness. To be more explicit: Theology, a phase of sacerdotalism, may be an absorbing study. Scholars may spend a lifetime pondering over the religions of the world, and they may accumulate a great knowledge concerning the beliefs of man. theology has an aspect as history, as art, as science, as literature, as discipline. All of these are considerations within the intellectual grasp; part of the mystery of the mind reaching out to know, yet it is obvious that this is not all of theology. Because there is theology as devotion, as experience, as atonement, as the inflowing into Self of spiritual impulses. Also, theology as gentleness; kindliness, thoughtfulness, veneration, adoration, humility.

All feelings are the polarized shadows of thoughts. Each feeling has its intellectual equivalent; each thought its emotional overtone. To understand this, to realize it, and practice it, is called right compassion. It is acceptance into Self of the dominion of the hollow square. It is realization as emotion, and emotion as realization.

Wherever there is a fact, it is an intellectual truth and satisfies the mind; but also it is emotional truth, and satisfies the heart. The mind would possess the fact; the heart would be possessed by the fact.

In the *Song which is Solomon's,* the mind says: "My beloved is mine." And the heart answers: "I am my beloved's." Between these two eternally sits the principle of transcendent and complete bliss, Asia's perfect Buddha, the power that knows and can discover within the depths of itself the blending of the seeker and the sought.

Do not try to think this through all at once. Do not attempt to feel the entire mystery. Try in some measure, however, to approach a little reverently the mysterious throne of peace on which sits together the three lotus-born lords of the Law. See not images, but powers; and meditate upon their mystery. To do this is to become wise in those things which come first among all the values of life.

If the intellect fails outwardly, without the balancing power of the emotions failing inwardly, the result is the materialist, whose mind is caught in the net of Mara. To feel devoutly without thought is to verge toward excess of the senses and passions, which ends in the total embrace of *Yama,* the fantastic creature of uncontrolled desires. Always there must be equilibrium; always there must be realization of the good Law; always the disciple must walk the Middle Path, balancing each extension of the consciousness with its proper *shakti* or consort.

In the religious philosophy of Asia all of the divinities, with the exception of the Supreme Power, the Absolute Itself, are represented as twofold. Each of the masculine divinities has its attendant female energy which is called the *shakti,* or goddess, or consort. This is to remind the disciple that every intellectual impulse must have its equivalent emotional reflex. All that flows out must flow back. All that comes forth must return. All that is learned must be used. All that is believed must be proved. All that is possessed must in time possess. Everywhere the Law operates through a balanced triad of energies—the Law, its operation, and its reaction.

In the doctrine of realization man first discovers through searching, and then through experiencing that which he has discovered as an emotional impregnation of consciousness. The ancients represented the spiritual awakening as a quickening and form of giving life, a conception within the Self. That which is conceived must be brought to birth. Knowledge that is discovered must bear fruit in action. All that we know and gain through knowing must be harvested to become that which we are. This is the Law.

RESTATEMENT OF PRINCIPLES

IT may be helpful at this point to review and restate the fundamental premises upon which this entire book is based. The attempt is to teach the disciplines of realization by the direct method of creating moods or conditions of consciousness for the student as he proceeds. Instead of presenting a series of formulas, the misapplication of which might lead to disastrous misunderstanding, the aim is to direct the realization by the Socratic mode of inferences. The student performs the exercises by the actual process of contemplating step by step the mystery of realization itself. He learns the processes by experiencing, in part at least, the conditions of the meditative life. After all, it is the purpose of esoteric exercises to release consciousness and direct its flow toward Truth.

Most metaphysical schools follow set formulas and attempt to unfold the consciousness of their students by the regular practice of mental exercises. Experience has demonstrated that such procedure is likely to lead to an intellectual acceptance of truths, not an actual experiencing of these truths. If a mental acceptance is regarded as sufficient, the disciple is already off the Path. Man evolves not by memorizing, but by experiencing as inner reality the sacred laws of being. This experiencing is an entirely personal adjustment. There is no possibility of limiting it by such equations as time, or place, or formula.

Realization is a readjustment of the *whole life* to a new and enlightened understanding of the reason for living. The perfect discipline, therefore, is a continuous flow of understanding; a process of growing by doing, of becoming by being. If you grasp this you will have the keys to the lesson we are trying to teach. You will find the normal application of the instruction in the adjustments of daily life. It is hoped that you will find all actions which you perform richer in meaning, deeper in significance, and more closely related to the larger pattern of universal purpose. The true meditation is the continuous living of enlightenment as the result of increasing internal inspiration.

The simple foundation already recommended is that a time be set aside for the practice of experiencing inwardly the beauties of the Law. No other actual discipline is necessary at this time. As realization unfolds it reveals to you the next step that you should take. The revelation is gradual, gentle, and understandable. There can be no conflict; progress moves upon the current of consciousness. What we know, we do. If on the other hand we try to grow merely from a moral sense of duty, development is arduous and difficult and the inner life is filled with contradictions resulting from inhibition and frustration. To attempt to perform a spiritual action when the will is not sustained by an adequate realization results in discord and internal inharmony.

Many students of esotericism permit the disciplines to become tasks. They perform them from a sense of spiritual responsibility, continuously prodding themselves toward virtuous action at the same time that their impulses are impelling them in a different direction. Take for example a simple virtue such as the control of the temper. Most spiritual-minded people realize the need for a placid disposition. When the conditions which arise in the physical environment are trying and irritating, the conscientious disciple attempts to meet the aggravations of the day with the virtue of self-control; even though the natural impulse is to become irritated the will restrains any outward display. It is a very human desire to be angry; it is a struggle then to hold the temper in check. This constant conflict between a high code of ethics and the difficulty of applying that code is detrimental to the nervous system; it leads to frustration and neuroses.

This is the reason why it is inadvisable and philosophically unsound to establish fixed standards, expecting disciples to abide by these standards regardless of the degree of their personal understanding. The solution to the problem is essentially Platonic. Human society has established certain material laws to protect man from irrational depredations, and all disciples must obey these laws. If you build from within outward, you remove the element of conflict. As realization unfolds you proceed to the performance of right action. When you understand life, temper dies within you. Anger slowly fades out, not immediately but gradually, as realization increases. A right action never is completely performed until it bears witness to the entire nature. *The virtue flows from the understanding. No self-control is necessary because the Self is controlling the action.*

The old axiom that the spirit is willing but the flesh is weak is not philosophically sound. The flesh is never either strong or weak. The term flesh merely applies to the impulses which are contrary to the code of spiritual action. A good deed is not to be performed in spite of ourselves, or in spite of part of ourselves, but for the reason that realization has caused us to be impelled to that good deed because it bears witness to *all* of ourselves.

This is what the ancients meant by the study of esthetics. The *beautiful* is the proper way of performing the *good.* Realization is the basis of beautiful action. All ulterior motives such as spiritual ambition and the desire to be good have ceased. Then, and then only, is virtue normal. Right action, in turn, reveals the future of itself. Each right action performed establishes the foundation for future right action, and reveals the direction in which this action should proceed. Thus realization is said to flow. It moves upon and within itself, and is its own impulse. Realize this and you cannot fail in the accomplishment of any good thing.

MULTIPLICATION OF THE METAPHYSICAL PERSONALITY

IN Taoist symbolism we have considered the method by which the Transcendental Being has been formed, and also how this being emerges from the material personality during contemplation. Also we have learned that the Transcendental Being energizes its *chhayas* or shadows so that seven conditions, called by the Buddhists *Dhyana Buddhas,* have been projected from itself. Each of these, in turn, has released its subordinate powers or genii, resulting in the establishment of a transcendental, mirror-like overshadowing of the material personality. Meditate upon this mystery and you will realize that it corresponds exactly with the esoteric systems of cosmogony, preserving the integrity of the the great law of analogy.

Now to continue with the mystery of experiencing the multiplications which take place within the structure of the Transcendental Being.

Realization unfolds like the body of the lotus. The

THE TRANSCENDENTAL FOUNDATIONS PERSONIFIED AS SEVEN ARHATS RELEASE THE ORDERS OF THE GENII

IN THE FOLLOWING SEQUENCE: THOUGHT ENGENDERS THE THINKER, AND FROM THE THINKER FLOW THE THOUGHTS

body swells and expands from within itself; gradually the petals open until the perfect flowering is accomplished—there is one flower with many petals. In the magical doctrines of Shingon Buddhism each of the petals is ornamented with the proper character and Sanskrit letter representing the power and mode of the Law. The thousand-petaled lotus of esoteric symbolism represents the magnificent diversity which bears witness to the absolute unity of life. All living creatures are like petals on the great flower of the Law. The golden heart of the lotus, the pure Law itself, is inconceivable and unapproachable by mortal consciousness. Yet as the life of the flower is revealed through the symbol of its blossom, so the perfection of the Law is made knowable through its radiant extensions which permeate all time and space.

As realization increases within the disciple, his consciousness unfolds like the sacred flower; innumerable petals open and realization must contemplate all of these extensions and yet preserve in the midst of them its own steadfastness. In the thronelike heart of the lotus, the meditating Buddha is "seated" in the midst of its own powers. When this state has been achieved the disciple has become an arhat.

This, then, is a problem in the realization of right administration. It has been written that when a man is faithful in small things, he shall be given dominion over greater things. As we put our smaller lives in order, a greater life unfolds to challenge us. When we have realized a few of the aspects of Reality, we become aware of more numerous aspects. Realization must rise to meet the challenge of the unknown. Therefore realization eternally must increase. Everything that we learn reveals more to be learned. Every virtue practiced reveals more virtues to be attained. Every truth comprehended becomes the starting point for the apprehension of greater truths.

How foolish, then, are those little mortals who believe they can possess all knowledge by some magical formula. As Sir Edwin Arnold has so beautifully written: "As veil upon veil we lift, we find veil upon veil behind." Each new problem to be realized releases a new principle of realization within ourselves. The Transcendental Being, for this reason, is represented as emanating innumerable specialized energies, each of which is appropriate to the realization of one of the extensions of universal Law. These specialized personalities are variously symbolized among the religions of the world.

In Buddhism they are the lohans, the five hundred singing priests who went forth to chant the Law. The lohans traveled to all parts of the world to carry the doctrine (realization) to all the creatures that abide in the directions of Space.

The disciple must realize as an inward experience the emanation of the lohans. From the Transcendental Being emerges the procession of the singing arhats. Visualize, if you can, this mystery taking place within yourself. Conjure up the form of the Transcendental Being. Realize it as polarized above your earth, as the sacred city of Shamballah floating in Space above the northern pole of the earth. Visualize the Transcendental Being seated in meditation and holding the golden pagoda of the heart in its hand. (This is a little temple held in the lap of the meditating figure.) As you watch with the eye of consciousness the door of the pagoda opens, and the Transcendental Being by the operation of will and yoga is releasing its arhats. From the open gateway of the golden shrine descends the sacred procession of the singing lohans. Each is depicted in the simple yellow robe of the monk. Slowly the procession moves down the temple steps, and each lohan, in turn, steps off into the air with hands clasped in prayer, floating away like some saffron colored bird, each in a different direction, chanting the Law, until finally the five hundred have gone forth. In the silence of meditation the chanting sounds ever more distant as the sweet singers journey out to the far places of the world of thought and Truth.

From that time on the disciple is ever aware that the singing priests are being witness to the Law. Whenever he becomes truly silent the disciple can hear their song, distant like an echo, but always floating on the inner air of the Self. As his realization increases the disciple can at will unite his consciousness with each of the lohans. They are the centers of himself in Space. As he can send conscious impulses along the nerves of the body, so he can send conscious impulses along the invisible nerves of his soul. Wherever one of the lohans builds his hermitage, there the disciple can experience the Law.

But this is not the end. As time goes on the student's realization increases until he can experience and realize with all of the lohans at one time. So perfectly does his realization flow that there no longer is any separateness in it. From the one Transcendental Being the many have gone forth. Through realization all the many are established again in the One. Thus it is that man has a thousand eyes, the eye of realization within himself. He has five hundred voices—all the lohans are singing his song, and he is singing their song. Gradually through realization we achieve union with the song that all life is singing.

In Eastern symbology there are many tales of the adventures of the lohans. They tell of saints that walk upon the waters, and of saints that fly through the air; there are lohans who have learned the language of the trees, and others that have preached their sermons to the birds. Some of the lohans live among the beauties of the forest, and others have built their huts on the sites of rocky hills. Some have preached to the stones so that the stones have lived; others have gone into the market place to bring the Law to the shopkeeper and the merchant. A few have entered into the presence of kings and have become the councilors of princes. Thus is symbolized the fact that all experience and all life is revealed through realization. Wherever the lohans go he teaches. Wherever realization flows, it reveals. This is a mystery of the Law.

An Eastern sage once told his disciple that if he could become still enough, gentle enough, and wise enough, he could hear the chanting of the Law everywhere. As the disciple did not seem to understand, his old master held up his hand and in a few seconds a little bird flew out of the forest and perched on the arhat's finger. As it sat and sang, the master asked: "Do you hear the song?"

The disciple answered: "Yes, I am aware of an exquisite melody."

"Be more silent and listen more intently," commented the master.

The disciple became still and sought to unite his consciousness with the consciousness of the bird. After a little while the master asked: "What do you hear now?"

The disciple replied: "I hear a little fluttering noise,

The arhat nodded approval. "You have reached that degree of silence in which you are hearing the beating of the little bird's heart. Now listen even more closely."

The disciple remained silent again until the master asked: "What do you hear now?"

The disciple turned a radiant face to his teacher. "Master, I have heard a miracle."

The arhat replied: "Explain it to me."

"I cannot explain it," answered the disciple. "All I know is that as my realization became one with the heart of the bird the sound of the beats changed into a song so subtle, so gentle that even the ears of realization could scarcely hear it. But as I listened with my soul and heart the sound became more and more clear, until at last the words were distinct."

"What were the words?" asked the master.

"They were the words of our most holy order," replied the disciple, "that the heart of the little bird was singing. *I take my refuge in the Law.*"

NINTH REALIZATION

This, then, is the ninth realization. The heart of all that lives is singing the Law. We may hear it in the rustle of trees, in the ripple of water. It rises as a chant from the confused sounds of the market place, and it floats in the silence over desert and mountain. It is the voice of the singing lohans, the realizations that have taken up their abode in the consciousness of all living things.

To our mortal perceptions there are wars, hates, and crimes; there is self-consciousness, greed, avarice, and ambition. But if realization takes us deeper into life,

further into the heart of things, we find beneath all that lives and within all that loves, that the rhythmic beat of the song is there. If we have the consciousness to understand the realization, to unite our lives with other lives, we shall hear the song in the heart of all existing creatures everywhere in Space. And they all sing the same song:

I TAKE MY REFUGE IN THE LAW.

X

APPROACH TO SPIRITUALITY

THE power of the imagination in the mental and emotional life of man has already been referred to. It is important to understand that the imaginative faculty is closely associated with and may be the direct cause of a kind of pseudo mysticism. A confusion of imagination and wishful thinking will result in what appears to be genuine spiritual development. Unless a student is protected during the first years of his development he is quite likely to become involved in the illusions of the astral light, the imaginative sphere.

While the disciple is attempting to release consciousness without the protection of an experienced teacher, constant vigilance is necessary. Such vigilance is impossible without a reasonable degree of knowledge of the structure of the visible and invisible worlds, and a very real appreciation of the laws governing them.

Carefully selected reading material is very helpful; recommended to the thoughtful aspirant is *Esoteric Buddhism* by A. P. Sinnett. This is a simple and useful handbook dealing with a wide variety of subjects, all directly related to the adjustment of the contemplative life to the cosmic pattern. The book is inexpensive, and it can be found in most public libraries.

It is not to be supposed that the study of such a text commits the student to the Buddhist religion. The true mystic progresses rapidly through the illusion of sects and creeds. He soon arrives at the realization that in the enlightened spiritual life there is no place for religious prejudice. Gradually he accepts the contributions of all religions, recognizing the universality of Truth.

Reading, however, has its hazards. The mind, confronted with new ideas, or new interpretations of already accepted ideas, naturally inclines to a kind of enthusiasm which stimulates the imaginative faculty; and the student rushes toward conclusions which may or may not be justified by the known facts. So again, there must be constant vigilance lest reason be compromised.

The practice of esoteric disciplines over a period of time normally results in an increasing sensitiveness to spiritual values. This sensitiveness may or may not result in extrasensory perceptions.

Generally it is better if the development is not accompanied by a noticeable extension of psychical powers. It is very difficult for the novice to estimate the true value of extrasensory perceptions. The tendency is to overestimate their importance, and consequently to overestimate the degree of development. This overestimation, combined with imagination and enthusiasm, can prove disastrous.

The resulting disaster may take one of several forms. Overwhelmed by a little progress, the student may regard himself as very highly advanced. When wishful desiring is added to this state of affairs, the novice falls into a vicious circle of imaginary illuminations and initiations, which will undermine him spiritually, and nullify any legitimate progress he may have made.

Many metaphysical movements have been founded by such enthusiasts—with detrimental results to themselves and others. Numerous so-called teachers of "higher truths" emerge from such psychic chemistry and support fantastic doctrines with the utmost sincerity. Most members of the metaphysical aristocracy with which the entire field of mysticism is plagued are the products of their own imaginations or of the wishful thinking of these so-called teachers.

Reflect seriously upon these facts and strengthen your resolution against the natural temptations arising from imagination and enthusiasm. True progress should be earnestly sought after, and as earnestly protected once there is evidence that some advancement has been achieved.

Spirituality should be approached calmly and maintained calmly. It is as dangerous to overestimate progress as it is to underestimate it. No intelligent student wishes to assume the karma for leading others into error. We are responsible for the results of teaching that which is untrue. Therefore we should instruct only to the degree that we ourselves have been instructed.

The primary purpose of this book is instruction in the release of the power of realization through the medium of the personality. If you have read carefully you have already discerned the difference between realization as an awareness through consciousness, and that pseudo realization which is merely an intellectual conception.

To make this extremely delicate point as certain as possible, let us review the matter from several different angles. Even though you may be convinced that you understand the subject correctly, it will be profitable to reflect upon these observations, and so satisfy yourself that no element of error has insinuated itself into your understanding. A slight error in the beginning, uncorrected, may become a great fault as you proceed.

An intellectual statement of a fact is properly termed an affirmation. That which is affirmed may be believed honestly, mentally accepted, and practiced as a virtue; and yet it may not be a realization. This is subtle; difficult to grasp accurately. So—an affirmation is platitudinous unless it leads immediately and directly toward realization. In fact it is far wiser not to affirm at all, but to reverse the process.

For example: It is an intellectual fact acceptable to all enlightened persons that the world, its laws, and the universal life that sustains it, are good. To reason from such an assumption—for even a fact must remain an assumption until it be experienced—may prove satisfying to the consciousness and result in a mental and emotional condition of well-being. Yet the person who believes in the fact that the world is good can become a menace to himself and to society. The affirmation of the essential virtue of life itself can lead to a static condition; to a fantastic effort to deny obvious faults and evident failings. It can result in a denial of experience and a refusal to acknowledge and to accept the challenge of progress. Or it may cause the student to attempt to advance spiritually by means of a series of affirmative impulses. He may believe that he is improving because he is affirming good in various concerns wherein that good is not apparent. Each affirmation seems a victory, and the enthusiastic affirmer plunges headlong into a condition of autohypnosis, scattering affirmations throughout space. Formulas, for him, become facts; the will to affirm becomes a substitute for internal enlightenment.

True realization differs not only in the method of approach, but in the technique of application over a long period of time in a wide variety of experiences. Realization does not imply an affirmation as to the goodness of the world. Rather, as the student grows in realization the consciousness *discovers* the goodness of the world as inner experience. The fact emerges from a contemplation of life; it is not imposed upon life. That which emerges and becomes evident manifests as a kind of growing thing. It is a living growth through the appearance of things. It is as unnecessary for the mind to restate to itself that the world is good as it is to tell oneself that a plant is growing.

Realization is a kind of seeing of which it may truly be said that "seeing is believing." The world is discovered as good, and the experience of this discovery results in an inward orientation of the life. Realization is a recognition both of the good in the world, and the world in the good. Furthermore, it is the sustained desire to be like the good, to serve good, and to become the good. Even as one reflects, these indivisible impulses cause consciousness to flow toward the normal object of its devotion. Thus the world is known as the *Good;* the forces which sustain it are known as the *Beautiful;* and the principle which ensouls it is known as the *One*—not formed, but known; not conjured up by the intellect, but revealed through understanding.

Realization can not be tinged with emotionalism. Religion, as interpreted in the lives of most people, is a series of emotional experiences in which feeling dominates and conditions the fact. As the mind can affirm goodness, emotion can affirm it by a series of pleasure reflexes. These include violent desires to possess the universal good, and such devotional reflexes as comfort, pleasure, happiness, security, and similar satisfying moods. These have their origin not in the more profound parts of the Self, but in the superficial emotional structure. They are a kind of smugness which, if encouraged, will lead to inertia. They are compensations for the disquietudes of mortal vicissitudes; escapes from the strains of conflict.

Pythagoras taught that irrationality manifests through two extremes or polarities. Man, while unenlightened, is a creature of extremes pacing back and forth behind the limitations of his personality. The intellect urges him from one extreme of attitude to another, and the emotions describe a similar arc from opposite to opposite. The mind, worried by the evils of the world which it has not been able to understand, searches eagerly toward a belief that all the world is good. The emotions, sensitive to the discords of human strife, quickly embrace any escape mechanism which teaches the reality of comfort and harmony. Thus life is made up of alternation between hope and hopelessness, optimism and pessimism, attachment and detachment, good and evil.

Pythagoras taught that realization was not to be discovered at either extremity of human impulse, but that Reality abode in the median plane in the center between all extremes. Truth must be sought in balance—not in unbalance. The natural impulses by their frantic searching lead not to Truth, but to the compounding of error.

Seeking neither to escape from evil nor to embrace good, the sage in contemplation releases realization through himself, and in the temperate central zone of consciousness proceeds without undue haste or unnecessary delay directly toward the Real. As the motion of universal Reality moves through him, he moves upon it as the singer's voice flows upon his breath.

Realization should not result in any visible emotional reflex. There should be neither pain nor ecstasy. Rather, there should be an increasing placidity visible as an intangible kind of strength, a strength without force, power without strain, and activity without stress.

Once achieved, realization is not easily lost. But it can be dominated by the mind and emotions if egotism is permitted to remain in any part of the pattern. A learned Brahman lived so nobly and so wisely, so runs the story, that after death he was carried directly to Indra's heaven; and there he found himself one of a select group of extraordinary souls. The honor that had been conferred for his previous merits was so great that the poor Brahman's head was entirely turned. He exclaimed in rapture that he was thankful that he was so much better than ordinary men. No sooner had this thought entered his mind than he felt himself being pitched out of Indra's heaven and falling with the speed of lightning to the lowest stratum of the purgatorial sphere.

As the growing plant may be destroyed by an unseasonal frost, so the unfolding realization cannot survive any immoderate mental or emotional complex. Imperceptibly, under a false stimulus, the realization is undermined; it shifts back to the status of opinion, affirmation, or emotion. The disciple, often unaware of what has occurred, has thus impeded his own progress. The surest symptom by which he may discover that error is entering into his realization is the diminution of his placidity. When he loses poise, he has lost realization.

REALIZATION IN ACTION

AS realization flows through the personality it causes certain definite changes in the objective life of the student. These changes must be observed because they constitute the clearest indication of true spiritual progress. If these physical and tangible changes are absent, then the realization is imperfect. All causes produce effects consistent with themselves. Unfolding consciousness must normalize and make temperate the courses of personal action.

In the doctrine of Buddhism *right action* is one of the eight spokes of the "wheel of the Law." According to the Buddhist canon right action is action proceeding from the realization of the Law. It is conduct under Law whereby the life of the student is directed by inner impulses rather than by outward impact. The Self dominates action.

Realization refines and sensitizes the codes of personal conduct. The enlightened individual manifests a sensitivity, a gentleness, and a simplicity in his actions which contrast clearly with the standards of less evolved types. There is no realization without action. And to the enlightened person there can be no action without realization.

It has been my observation that the study of metaphysical subjects is not sufficient in itself to alter in any marked degree the standards of personal action. Students who have given the best years of their lives to reading and research still exhibit distressing symptoms of misunderstanding and ignorance. There is no virtue in affirming the possession of spiritual graces unless these attainments are evident in the natural reflexes of thought and emotion. To claim enlightenment and to practice criticism and intolerance is to deny with proof that which has been affirmed without proof. In such cases it is apparent that realization does not exist. Perfection is not expected; but there must be a definite evidence of improvement to substantiate any assumption of growth.

As realization unfolds it produces a natural sensitivity which cannot endure conflict within the personality. In the terms of Plotinus, the harmonies within the Self verge toward the harmonies of the world. It does not follow that realization produces a supersensitivity to the problems of the outer ilfe. The true mystic does not expect to change his world, but he does demand harmony within his own personality. The student who cannot meditate because his family, or his friends, or his environment are unsympathetic, takes this attitude because he is without realization. True realization demands no change in others, but insists upon certain standards for the self.

Realization produces a marked refinement in the tastes, inclining the mind and the emotions toward an appreciation of beauty and nobility. It does not, however, demand possession in order to satisfy the appreciation. The East Indian mystic, beholding a lotus, sees in it the symbol of his whole spiritual aspiration; and reveres it for its beauty of design, its color, and the spiritual truths and laws which it symbolizes. Yet he does not desire to pick the lotus, or to make it his own. He is perfectly content to remain a little way off and to meditate upon its mystery.

The proof of refinement is thoughtfulness. We may define thoughtfulness as a gentle and sincere consideration of any matter.

Thoughtfulness also involves the factor of anticipation. The thoughtful action is one performed when the need is recognized, rather than when demanded by pressure or expedience. Thoughtfulness is one of life's overtones; something added to the necessity, by which utility is beautified and ennobled. It is not the performance of action as duty, but of action as privilege.

The presence of thoughtfulness indicates the extension of realization toward the object of the thoughtfulness. This results in another of the Buddhist articles of virtuous living.

One of the eight parts of the path to the Real is defined by the articles as *right thoughtfulness.* This term is far more dignified, richer in meaning, than the term right thinking. Meditate upon the difference and you will realize that right thinking can be merely intellectual; but right thoughtfulness is understanding released through thinking.

This book has earlier emphasized the mystical significance of appreciation as one of the greatest powers of the soul. Now associate appreciation with right thoughtfulness. The result of combining these forces is *right veneration.*

Never interpret veneration as a mere acceptance of the sanctity of some object, person, or belief. Veneration is much more. It is a gentleness toward all life; a realization of the intrinsic nobility in all living things. It does not cause the disciple to fall on his knees in blind adoration. Rather, it inspires a desire to love, to serve, and to protect all life.

It would seem obvious that with such forces stirring within the personality and its sensory extensions, marked changes should be evident even to the uninformed. Therefore, we say that realization moderates all courses of action and becomes, in a sense, visible through the changes which it produces in visible and recognizable consequences.

The Orient places the highest stamp of approval upon evidence of realization in action. Whereas the West rewards activity according to the measure of its intensity, the East honors action in terms of its quality. The Westerner is termed active if he appears to be in a continuous state of motion and agitation. The cause of the agitation and the direction of the motion are seldom considered. The Oriental regards agitation with definite distrust; and motion without direction as a total loss. The performance of unnecessary action is recognized as a proof of ignorance. Realization, because of the gentleness of its inherent nature, never impels to violent consequences. It never leads to abrupt, disconnected action. It does not produce contradictions, and never inspires intolerance.

Reason stimulates observation—which may be defined as *right seeking,* another of the Buddhist virtues. Observation is a perception of values. Here again the average Westerner is poorly informed. He has been trained to be impressed by mass and grandeur. He is unduly influenced by size, and number, and proximity. His attention is stimulated by the imminent; he sees first that which is nearest in place rather than that which is greatest in quality. Through realization the consciousness becomes aware of the dignity of that which is scarcely perceptible to the outward senses. Truth, locked within form, manifests only in part according to the development of form. Observation is man's power to perceive the degree of realization manifested through the forms about him.

Each of the arts of Asia has a tradition which has been enriched by centuries of observation. The artist is rewarded by being understood by those equal to himself or superior to him in realization. An Oriental art dealer once showed me the treasure of his store. Each dealer usually has some treasure which he does not greatly desire to sell, but which he keeps to show those who will appreciate it. In this instance it was a lacquered box carefully wrapped in silk and cloth, according to the Eastern fashion. He explained that it had been years since he had unwrapped the box. Within the wrappings there was a glorious, jewel-like perfection of the lacquerer's art. He opened the box. Within, a little tray occupied the upper half of the space.

Removing it, he explained: "You will perceive that there are no cleats on the inside of the box to support the weight of the tray. It is so perfectly fitted that it is sustained on compressed air. Yet it is capable of being weighted with such objects as might normally fill the box without falling to the bottom. It has been floating thus for ten years. Consider that this box is made of wood and therefore subject under normal conditions to expansion and contraction, and to the effects of dampness, yet it has not warped even a thousandth of an inch. This box was made by one of the greatest lacquer experts more than a hundred years ago. In all that time the tray has never stuck and has never loosened."

He placed the tray back in the box and suggested that I press it slightly with my hand. I did so, and it bounced as on a cushion, but it did not fall to the bottom.

By this time the dealer had reached a pitch of enthusiasm beyond which his Buddhist philosophy would not permit him to go. But he had to dissertate a little more on the subject of the treasure of his store.

"The box with its floating tray may appear to be the product merely of ingenuity or skill. But it is more than that. It is a monument to patience. It bears witness to an impulse within the consciousness to do all things perfectly, the impulse to put the most of one's ability into every action. It reveals that the artist understands the dignity of action; it must bear witness to his best effort; it must reveal the inward desire that each action should glorify the Self in the story it tells. When the action is adequately and completely performed, it has been a kind of worship. We honor Truth by performing Truth. We reveal the Law by adequate action.

"Furthermore, those who see this box have an opportunity to share the realization of its designer. It is beautiful in all of its parts, bearing witness to the beauty of understanding which created it. It is perfect in all its parts, revealing that the technique of the designer was adequate to the expression of his inward realization. Therefore, my friend, this is art. Art is the understanding to create perfectly, combined with the skill to express."

Reverently, gently, as he might handle some fragile living thing, the shopkeeper returned the box to its wrappings and placed the treasure of the house in its obscure place. With a little sigh he went back to the daily tasks, murmuring: "I wonder if I shall open that package again before I die."

This is a problem in right observation; to see not only the wonderful, but to feel the impulse which created the wonderful; not to be so much amazed by skill as to be moved by the realization of what was necessary that skill might exist. Thus, appreciation combined with observation produces the gentle veneration present in the manner and words of the little shopkeeper.

How few there are in the world who could really understand the message of the lacquer box! Only a consciousness which has evolved its own creative understanding could sense the mystic communion with Truth that was symbolized by the simple perfection of this exquisite piece of lacquer work. It would have meant much to Michelangelo, who knew that trifles make perfection. But only understanding can understand.

The degree of realization which the student achieves in the studies of the mystical can be determined in part by his reactions toward the exquisite and the fine. If he still prefers the bric-a-brac with which the uninformed surround themselves, to the dignity of the blank wall, it is evident that realization is lacking.

Take a man into an art gallery and ask him to point out the picture that he likes best. It will then be possible to tell the degree of his understanding. It will not be a measure of his technical knowledge of art, but of his internal reaction to the pictorial. Study the habits of human beings, and most of all, your own habits. By observing your reactions and reflexes you can determine with certainty whether what you fondly believe to be spiritual expansion is merely an intellectual conception.

Realization as conduct is the performing of Truth. Realization as observation is the perceiving of Truth. Realization as appreciation is the enjoyment of Truth.

Realization as speech is the utterance of Truth. Realization as meditation is the contemplation of Truth. Realization as veneration is the acceptance of Truth in a spiritual mystery. Discipline as Truth is obedience to the Law. And sight as Truth is the discovery of Reality in form, line, color, and composition.

Thus we have a measure of checking to make sure that our realization is not illusional. If we are honest with ourselves we know the degree of actual growth which we have accomplished. We know, without being told, the degree to which our tempers have subsided and our irritabilities have been subdued. We know the measure of our honesty and the degree of our integrity—at least approximately. If after several years of metaphysical study these temperamental qualities have not changed markedly for the better, we are not studying correctly, regardless of what others may say or how good our memories have become. We have no real understanding unless our lives are better in practical terms. We have a poor memory indeed if we cannot remember the laws of life. If memory does not sustain its continuity so that the thing remembered becomes the thing done, little has been gained.

TENTH REALIZATION

A flowing of understanding into action as Truth within the individual is released through realization. Let it be understood as impelling to conduct identical with its own nature. Practice the disciplines of the Law. Know the Law in the motion of your thinking. Feel the Law in the quality and directing of your emotions. Express the Law through the rhythm and co-ordination of your actions.

During periods of meditation practice simply at first, and later with greater diversity of application, the experience of the Law. Place before you on the table a simple but significant object, preferably something small and fine; something that you greatly prize. During the process of realization, and with the consciousness rather than with the mind, extend your hand and pick up the object. Observe this simple motion. As your realization increases, the action of picking up an object will become symbolical of the entire development of your consciousness. You will find that the impulse will slowly change from a muscular reflex to a motion rich with meaning and rhythm impelled by definite understanding, clearly purposed, and executed with exquisite grace.

As your understanding increases, the motion toward picking up the object will bbecome slower and slower, until, like the Zen monk, you will be able to accomplish the action without movement, by realization alone. Philosophically, this is immovable motion. The object will be picked up by realization. This does not mean that the physical object will be levitated or will be carried to the person by mental power or any physically miraculous means. It implies, rather, that the reality of the object, the significance, and the purpose which are its real self, will be picked up by the consciousness of the meditating individual without actually being moved at all.

As realization extends throughout the departments of life the simple act of picking up something will become symbolic of all motions. First it will be beautified; a grace and harmony will be conferred upon action, and gradually coarse action will practically cease, all action being performed within realization.

XI

ILLUMINATION

TO the mystic the word *illumination* means inward enlightenment. As the sun lights the physical world and sustains all life with its energies, so the Self, the spiritual sun, lights the inner world of spirit and preserves with its power the spiritual aspirations and ideals of mankind.

Many are the popular misconceptions about the metaphysical significance attached to the word illumination. Illumination is not to be interpreted as some kind of an external experience; it is an entirely natural consequence of living an enlightened life. Illumination does not confer perfection, nor does it bestow a sudden extension of spiritual powers. Rather, it is a kind of dawning within the Self, the beginning of a greater light, the *Aurora* of Jakob Boehme.

Illumination should never be interpreted as an acceptance into some elite body of initiated adepts, nor as an introduction into some arcane storehouse of secret lore. It has no association with fantastic pageantries, robed figures, priests and altars, soul flights, or similar absurdities so often suspected by the uninformed. Illumination is simply a process of awakening . . . of opening one's eyes, lifting another veil, opening another door . . . and looking toward the face of Truth. It is the consciousness having penetrated a little farther into the wonders of living.

There is no cause for pride in illumination—if anything, the illumined student becomes more gentle and more humble. But there is no groveling humility. The disciple approaches Truth because it is his birthright. He neither demands nor supplicates. He obeys the Law, fits himself to receive light, and the light comes.

Illumination is not a single experience marked by an abrupt transition from a state of ignorance to a state of wisdom. It is a series of related experiences, a series of spiritual discoveries. There will be moments that seem more radiant than others, but the whole experience will extend over a period of many lives. Growth is a sequence of unfoldment; an orderly procedure marked by the gradual increase of internal light.

The child in school struggles heroically with the mystery of the multiplication table. To him it is a mystery, and his mind is seeking to grasp the elements and principles which underlie the theory of multiplication. Weeks pass before the processes are mastered, and then the child suddenly realizes that it understands the workings of the multiplication table. No longer is there a mystery; the problem has been mastered. A secret inward flush of victory follows; a feeling that now the whole world is conquered. There is a new sense of strength and a new determination to attack other problems and to solve them. The flash of understanding in the young student's mind which solved the mystery of the multiplication table was a sort of illumination. It was consciousness becoming aware; some light flowing into the fumbling mind revealed the mystery.

In the schoolboy's flash of understanding there is something spiritual and mystical. If that inner light had not come he would have studied in vain. And without understanding, learning is useless. Yet never in wildest imagining would the schoolboy feel that he belongs to some secret order of superphysical beings merely because he mastered the principle of multiplication. Neither would he expect his new understanding to become a universal panacea for ignorance. What he does find out, and soon, is that after mastering the principles of multiplication, he must learn the rules of division. Here he is confronted with new principles and new procedures. Once more he must grope for the laws, and again he must find them within himself.

A little enlightenment does not bestow immunity from future effort, nor does it promise peace and security in some psychic summerland. There is nothing impractical about mysticism. The difficulty is that many impractical persons seek refuge in mysticism without making any effort to correct their own shortcomings.

REALIZATION AS ILLUMINATION

WE have learned that realization is a gradual extension of universal energy through the personality of the human being. Also we have learned that in order to become enlightened we must identify the personal consciousness with this universal force; then we may consciously participate in it and be moved by it as it moves through us. Wherever there is a point of contact between personal consciousness and universal consciousness, there is an extension of the personal consciousness. This extension is properly called illumination. As two electric wires brought together will produce a spark at their point of junction, so the meeting of the lesser and the greater selves is always accompanied by a temporary expansion of the lesser self. This flash of energy is interpreted through the personality of the human being in terms of the sudden extension of awareness. Something sought for is suddenly found; something desired is suddenly felt.

Illumination always takes the form of solution, solving the problem most imminent to the Self. The composer with his unfinished symphony, the artist with his unfinished canvas, the poet with his unfinished verses, and the scientist with his unfinished experiments—each of these is confronted with a problem; each has gone as far as he can proceed unaided. Having exhausted the resources of conscious personal knowledge, each is groping for a solution. It may require days, months, or even years to complete the unfinished task. Without realizing it each of these men is waiting for a miracle. Only a revelation; only some mystical extension of consciousness can make possible the completion of the work.

Then the light comes. How, no man knows; when, no man knows; why, no man knows. We do know, however, that effort is rewarded with accomplishment. That which we earnestly desire and honestly strive after will come. We may see the answer as in a dream; it may flash into our minds; it may leap out at us in the motion of the millstream, in the ripples of a pool, or in the flight of a bird. The clue may come from the thoughtless words of a friend, the notion of some mere acquaintance. But within the reason there is a little burst of awareness. The whole body and mind thrill with the acute knowledge that the answer is known; the solution is found. The experience of genius bears ample testimony that without consecration and perseverance there can be no illumination. It is a reward for effort; not a substitute for effort.

The philosophic life is in itself the noblest of all the arts. To live well is the supreme test of wisdom. It is impossible to perfect living without illumination. It is only in those moments of contact during which the Self is in part revealed that the purpose of life can be more adequately realized. There can be no enlightened living without a realization of the reason for living. This reason cannot be supplied by the intellect, nor can it be discovered by the senses. The true reason for our existence can be found only through communion with the Self. Only the Self knows its own purposes. As personal beings, we are merely shadows cast by the Self. As mortal creatures, we are the instruments by which the Self accomplishes its purposes. Illumination comes when the instrument begins to discover the reason for which it was fashioned.

Modern psychology has invented the term *mystical experience* to explain the mystery of illumination. Havelock Ellis, in summarizing the effect upon his life which was produced by a mystical experience occurring to him, wrote in substance: After this experience nothing seemed to matter any more. Everything was so supremely right, so entirely as it ought to be, that no longer was there any space for doubts, concern, or dissatisfaction.

Havelock Ellis had glimpsed the Law. For one brief second he had looked out through the window of his personal self into the greater world that lay beyond. Light had come within. The mood could not be sustained. In a fraction of a second it was gone, but the consequences of that mood were profound and lasting. No matter what he might say, no matter what others might say to him, no matter what conclusions might be reached by the "fifty jarring sects," Havelock Ellis was sustained by a personal experience. Others argued; he knew. Others wondered, hoped, and feared; but he had experienced a certainty. He could not convey that certainty to any other living creature. If others ridiculed or disapproved, he could not confer his understanding or convince them. The certainty was his own, but he could not share it. He could state it, but he had no power to force conviction.

To the earnest student, the desire for illumination may become a serious handicap. If you are too conscious of the ends you desire, you may become neglectful of the means by which you hope to achieve those ends. To exist from day to day longing to be illuminated is to fall almost certainly into the illusions of wishful thinking. If the longings stimulate the imagination, it will soon bring about pseudopsychic experiences which to the hopeful and imaginative soul assume the proportions of cosmic enlightenment.

Illumination can never come until the causes for it have been definitely established. It is the crowning effort. Do not wait for it. Do not hope for it. Do not wonder about it. Do not fear that it will not come. Develop realization; normalize and beautify life. And illumination will be the normal and natural consequence, not as a single episode; not one tremendous burst of enlightenment, but a steady release and increasing flow of understanding into and through the lower faculties of the reason.

It has often been pointed out that tension and effort are detrimental to spiritual progress. This is especially true in so abstract and sensitive a subject as illumination. The story is told of a Zen monk studying in Kamakura who practiced the disciplines daily for twenty years in order to earn for himself the merit of illumination. At the end of that time he was still untouched by the flame of the Self. Discouraged at last, he climbed to the top of a tall pagoda, determined to cast himself off. He had given up all hope. Having come to the final resolution and being utterly resigned, he flung himself from the pagoda. As he fell, realization came—and so great was the enlightenment that manifested through him that he landed unhurt at the foot of the tower. He immediately rushed to the abbot for an explanation of this phenomenon.

The old man listened gravely to the account, and then nodded his approval and understanding. "My son," he explained, "for these twenty years you have tried to force the Real. You have dominated that which will not obey the orders of any living thing. You have desperately striven to discover that which no man can discover. Truth must discover you. At last, having failed in all your efforts to grasp the formless aspect of light, you became utterly discouraged. You gave up. You relaxed. You tried no longer. In your very desperation you came to a state of peace. Life was purposeless without Reality. You no longer desired to live. For an instant all of your psychic organisms were calm. And in that instant the twenty years of your discipline bore fruit. The light came. You no longer plagued with the intensity of your own desires that which could come only during desirelessness."

Detachment is truly a part of the mystic disciplines. Too many beginners in metaphysical matters are longing after liberation. Too few are performing the disciplines of liberation. There is no liberation except through realization and illumination. These are the only escapes from the "wheel of the Law." Yet they are not really methods of escape. More correctly, they are the outgrowing of the limitations by which most mortals are afflicted. As birth is the only entrance into the physical life, so enlightenment is the only entrance into the spiritual life. However, we must not desire too intensely after spiritual release or we shall cheat ourselves out of some part of physical experience.

For the philosopher, "all things in good time." Without undue haste and without undue delay, without regret and without anxiety, the mind established in wisdom flows toward the Real. Under such conditions illumination is as natural as life itself. And only when it is entirely natural is it real. So-called illumination produced in any other way and by any other means can be but hallucination.

The disciple can protect himself in one regard. He can constantly ask himself whether the spirituality which he believes he has achieved is consistent with what he knows about his own spiritual integrity. If he seems to know more than he is, to be wiser than his virtues, to be more advanced than the standard of his thinking and living, then he certainly is deceiving himself. His progress is not real but imaginary, and he should set himself immediately to the task of correcting conditions before delusions further confuse him. We are not worthy of enlightenment merely because we desire it, but only when we have won it. And there are so few who are willing to earn. The masses expect nature to bestow its greatest gifts regardless of worthiness.

The contrast between the intellectual and the mystical viewpoint is exemplified by the meeting of Confucius and Lao-Tze. Confucius was a man possessing the highest mental and reasoning powers. Not only was his mind profound, but he retained to the end the delightful qualities of humor and curiosity that revealed intellectual superiority. His thought was profound, gentle, and dignified. He sought to educate China, and to release through the Chinese consciousness the noble traditions which had descended through centuries of scholarship and culture.

But Confucius was not a mystic. His spiritual nature never escaped the conventions of thought. He never denied mysticism, but admitted simply and honestly that he was unqualified to indulge in its abstractions. He honored the mystic, studied the mystical books, and even wrote commentaries upon some of them. His knowledge was encyclopedic, but it is doubtful if he ever experienced that conscious extension into participation with infinites which the mystic terms illumination. This does not mean that Confucius was unenlightened—and here is a fine distinction. The trained mind properly disciplined may arrive at the same conclusion that the mystic approaches through realization. The difference lies in the degree of conscious participation in the known. The intellectual approaches Truth as something possessing form and dimension outside of his own nature. But the mystic approach to Truth is that of consciousness finding itself as formless and dimensionless Reality.

A STONE RELIEF CARVING FROM THE HAN DYNASTY DEPICTING THE MEETING OF CONFUCIUS AND LAO-TZE. THIS FINE OLD STONE RUBBING SHOWS THE TWO IMMORTALS OF CHING EXCHANGING THE FORMALITIES OF GREETING AT THE ENTRANCE OF THE LIBRARY OF THE CHOU. THE ARTISTIC TREATMENT, THOUGH APPARENTLY CRUDE, IS REGARDED AS TYPIFYING ONE OF THE FINEST PERIODS IN CHINESE PRIMITIVE DESIGN

Lao-Tze, in his life, his teaching, and his personality, was completely the mystic. He moved through his world untouched by the literalisms of life. His scholarship was entirely within himself. He contacted the literature and art of his time without being in any way caught or entangled in the maze of their intellectual or emotional grandeur. He was in this world but never of it, dwelling always apart in the distant heights of his own realization. Somewhat older in years than Confucius, he was far older in spiritual understanding.

The mystical difference in age has been adroitly adapted by Taoist painters in depicting these two great men, as is illustrated by a fine old Chinese painting. It bears the title "Lao-Tze and the Infant Confucius." The great Taoist saint is sitting in the shadow of a great rock from which springs the ragged, twisted form of a storm-swept pine. Lao-Tze, represented as an aging man wrapped in a somber mantle, is gazing down with the benign serenity of a wise and loving parent at the babe he is holding in his arms. Confucius, with the intent, frank, and trusting expression so often seen on the faces of intelligent children, nestles securely in the old man's arms. The whole conception is noble and meaningful. It is unlikely that there is any historical foundation for the picture. It is a symbolical representation of the parenthood of realization as compared to intellectual accomplishment.

Much has been made of the traditional meeting of Confucius and Lao-Tze on the steps of the library of the Chou. It was on this occasion that Confucius described the spiritual accomplishment of Lao-Tze as being compared to a great dragon twisting and turning in space, flashing through clouds which obscured the mental lives of normal human beings. The dragon soared upward through all the states of being and then streaked downward into the very depths of matter; a great immeasurable spirit ascending and descending at will, flying free in space, unlimited by any mortal restraint. He could admire this free spirit, but he could not bring his own personal experience into rapport with so cosmic a consciousness.

To the Taoist the dragon represents illumination. It conveys to his mind the strange powers of the Real. It is the only creature in the Taoist mythological system that is entirely self-sustained, inhabiting the great field of Tao itself. The dragon is Space as consciousness. It dwells in the Absolute, moving back and forth with perfect freedom in the limitless vistas of Reality. Space, or Tao, is eternally moved by the tides of Law. Within it are all shapes, all forms, all motions. This mystery is expressed by representing universal extension as a sea of currents and energies filled with nebulous whirlings and patterns designed to express immense cosmic processes. Here, self-nourished and unique, one without a second, dwells the dragon, expressing in its form the infinite courage of realization which sustains itself in the mystic ocean of the universal Self.

Lao-Tze perceived instantly with mystical penetration that Confucius was incapable of the mystical comprehension. The men met, performed the formalities, conversed for a little time, and parted. Lao-Tze returned to the gray walls of his library, and Confucius to the secluded grove where he discoursed with his disciples.

There is no record of any opinion that Lao-Tze may have expressed as the result of his meeting with the greatest scholar of his time. But Confucius described to his disciples his impressions of Lao-Tze. He was profoundly affected, and sought earnestly to find some spirit of mysticism within himself. He had the greatness to recognize greatness, but not the realization to share in the lofty speculations of the initiated mystic.

This brings to consideration two important Taoist doctrines concerning illumination. The first is courage, and the second is sufficiency. Courage is understood to mean that strength of purpose by which the consciousness steadfastly approaches the Real. Here realization must support the quest. It is not sufficient to desire Truth. It is necessary to strengthen desire with the courage of conviction. Truth brings not only liberation, but undreamed of responsibilities to the Self. That which is realized becomes the absolute law of living. There can be no departure from inward reality. Once man knows, he must do, or else his knowledge will torture him. Failure to think, to act, and to live that which is realized, or any effort on the part of the lower nature to compromise realization produces a desperate conflict within the life.

It is an axiom that that which is realized is naturally performed. But we must remember that for the average person realization is imperfect, and the moments of conscious extension are separated from each other by relapses into what may be termed human interludes. Only the most highly evolved mystic who has devoted many lives to the unfoldment of the mystical disciplines within himself can continuously maintain his realization. The intermittent flashes of greatness, termed by the Taoists the "blinking of the dragon's eye," result in a material condition requiring a high measure of personal courage.

There must first be the courage and dedication to depart from the errors of other men and to devote the life to a reality which is beyond the understanding of associates and friends. Then there must be the courage to face the inevitable failures of good intentions. There must be realization deep and true enough to accept these backslidings without emotional intemperance. There must be no self-condemnation, no interludes of remorse, no periods of despair. Realization must be true enough to sustain the consciousness in tranquillity throughout success and failure which alternate in the life of the disciple. To lose tranquillity in what some feel to be the right aims of self-censure, is again to fall into error. As surely as there must be no spiritual ambition, so there must be no spiritual remorse.

The quest for the Real must become a continuous, gentle effort. All things in nature will accomplish realization in the fullness of time. Nothing can hasten Law. It is its own speed. Nothing can be delayed beyond the limitations imposed by the immaturity which is intrinsic to all mortal creatures.

The second Taoist doctrine concerning illumination emphasizes the necessity for sufficiency. The doctrine creates itself, sustains itself, abides by itself, moves impelled by its own nature, and has no home but Space. This attacks the fundamental human impulse toward dependency. Even religion subtly inculcates a doctrine of dependency. Man is ever searching for a strength outside of himself upon which he can cast his burdens.

Many persons studying mysticism are seeking for some source of security to which they can turn in time of trouble. This insufficiency has no place in a doctrine of realization. The dragon-soul abides only in the shadow of eternity itself. The illuminated consciousness must be completely self-sustaining, unaffected by any sense of aloneness.

As enlightenment increases, the desire to share it increases; but with this desire comes the realization that it is impossible to share the Real. Realization is an inward experience which can come only to those who have won it in their own right. It cannot be conferred. The impulses which realization bestows upon the personality will not be understood by others less developed.

Lao-Tze dwelt in the old libraries, wandering like a ghost up and down through the passageways, surrounded by thoughts of other men, yet untouched by those thoughts. In like manner the mystic, though bound physically to the life of his world, must understand the freedom of his inner life or he will be very much alone. A few will venerate him from afar, but none will understand him. Jesus, praying in the garden of Gethsemane, was alone. His disciples could not keep one vigil with him. Their realization could not go with him into the presence of the Father.

Realization brings with it sufficiency, but unless the growth toward it be entirely natural and unaffected by ambition the disciple will find it difficult to maintain sufficiency without leaning on some error for support. His realization will not be continuous enough in its earlier stages to prevent some conflict between the personal and impersonal phases of his life. He must recognize and realize the difference between freedom and aloneness The man who is alone has a certain freedom which he often fails to appreciate. The man who is free finds in his freedom an aloneness that is often difficult to bear. If such conflict arises it must be met by realization.

When realization is highly developed, time and place cease. Time and place are intimately involved in the pattern of relationships. When time and place have been absorbed by realization, then aloneness and distance are gone. As Confucius said of Lao-Tze's spirit: "Realization moves back and forth, up and down, in and out." The interlude of aloneness lies in the critical amount of adjustment between personal and universal consciousness. Universal consciousness cannot be alone because it is part of everything; it is a participation in life which forever precludes any acceptance of isolation. But this realization is not easily achieved.

It is because of certain great problems such as these that I have so carefully emphasized the necessity of developing realization by gentle and normal means. If the development be entirely correct, the motion of the consciousness will be so gradual and so normal that these abrupt interruptions will be passed through almost without incident. Universality will increase to the same degree that the personality decreases, with a corresponding decrease in stress and strain. If for any reason the effort at development is forced and the flow of consciousness is interrupted by mental or emotional complexes, then such problems as aloneness will inevitably manifest themselves.

If this occurs you should slow your forward motion and gather up the loose ends which enthusiasm or spiritual ambition has caused you to overlook. Proceed no further in the extension of some one part of your consciousness until your realization is sufficient to assure the continuity and normalcy of your living. Not to make such correction will result in misery and temporary failure. Your aloneness may cause you to rush ahead into unwise attachments or to falsely glorify as a spiritual virtue your sense of isolation. The latter course of action produces the hermit, the recluse, and the fanatic, who believe that there is some spiritual virtue in frustration. Such a course of action renders consciousness less suitable for normal realization, and usually ends in a stalemate.

From the foregoing it will become more evident how delicate are the adjustments which are necessary to a normal spiritual growth. When we realize that most students of mysticism are not even aware of the necessity for these adjustments, it is not difficult to understand why most of them turn out to be impractical and intolerant. It is not the failure of mysticism itself, but the failure of the disciple to bring to the subject an adequate background of general knowledge and normal viewpoint. Each must protect himself with his own understanding against what the unbeliever has rather appropriately termed "sickly mysticism."

It is unfortunate that the world has been trained to accept as virtuous, traits of character which are not necessarily superior. The Hindu holy man sitting on a bed of spikes gains a certain popular sanctity because he endures physical discomfort for his belief. It is perfectly proper to respect his sincerity, but not to admire his understanding. The same attitude is appropriate toward the Christian saints and religious leaders. To shorten one's life and to multiply one's sufferings may reflect devotion, but certainly such actions should not be set up as standards for normal spiritual development. The intention may be right, but the realization that is the true spiritual development must be comparatively slight.

It is much more appropriate to the ideals of mysticism to symbolize growth by a beautiful, spontaneous, happy unfoldment, like that of the opening flower, than to do so by an example of cruelty which would accomplish Heaven by afflicting its own body with a heartless despotism. So be not deceived by the standards of spirituality which others set up. Do not try to emulate the lives of others, even though they may have a high reputation for sanctity. Search for realization associated with beauty, gentleness, peace, and simple dignity. Spiritual progress is not to be achieved by any creed of cruel action, or by the heartless inhibition of normal impulses.

ELEVENTH REALIZATION

This realization is your contemplation of the mystery of illumination. Try to experience inwardly a sense of gentle awakening. Go out into the dawn and meditate upon the daily awakening of the world. See how the darkness gives way to a dim light which slowly spreads across the surface of the earth. Observe how this light gradually brings into life all the sleeping wonders of nature. Then the rising of the sun, its own rays reaching into the very consciousness of living creatures, until each stirs and again takes up the tasks of the day.

There is no conflict, no struggle. There is light in the world, and the acceptance of light—the acceptance of light as natural, as normal as the simple awakening of that which has known light and darkness before.

Illumination is a dawn within the Self. The light of the spirit brings into life the innumerable aspects of realization. An empire of effort awakens, and all life continues its search for peace.

XII

SUSPENSION OF THE OBJECTIVE MIND

AS the Buddhist disciplines lead to nirvana or absorption into the universal Self, and the Yoga philosophy teaches a union with universals through samadhi, so the Taoist doctrines of China have as their goal the identification of consciousness with Tao, the supreme principle of life.

To the Chinese understanding there are two modes or conditions of Tao—its relative and its absolute aspects. Every living creature at every step of its evolution participates to some degree in the mystery of Tao. This participation is relative adjustment; the partaking of Tao. In distinction to this continuous process of adjustment is the ultimate identification with Tao. All growing results in growth. All growth ends in Tao.

As absolute Tao is beyond definition, it cannot be contemplated by the intellect. It cannot even be attained by the mind. It may be symbolized, set up as a goal, recognized as an ultimate, yet it eludes definition. Tao is. This fact is the supreme reality which the mind is capable of framing. What Tao is can only be experienced through the mystical disciplines of realization and illumination.

When Lao-Tze departed from China, riding on his green water-buffalo, he stopped for a short time with the keeper of the northern gate of the great wall. It was on this occasion that he compiled the *Tao Te Ching,* his only literary production. This brief thesis, containing only five thousand characters, is the foundation of all Taoist metaphysical speculation. It is principally concerned with an effort to expound that which is knowable by the human intellect concerning the mystery of Tao. Having delivered this writing to the guardian of the northern gate, Lao-Tze rode off into the mysterious depths of the Gobi Desert and was never again seen by mortal eyes.

He left behind him the mysterious symbol of Tao as the Law, the Way, the Means, and the End—one comprehensive idea that embraces both the seeker and the sought, the means and the end. We live in Tao; we desire Tao; we attempt to understand Tao; we strive to become Tao; and at the end of all seeking, we are Tao.

It is evident that so mystical a speculation cannot be grasped by the mind which has been trained to the contemplation of formal and tangible matters. We lack the equipment to enable us to visualize in the abstract. To understand, we must bestow form and dimension. To formalize or limit Tao is a philosophical impossibility. Therefore it remains like the mysterious swirling clouds, a force and a principle realized yet not realized; its imminence is recognized as necessary, but unrecognizable in its very nature.

Buddha and Socrates both refused to attempt a definition of Absolute Being. Each gave the same reasons. In the first place it was impossible, and in the second place, even were it possible, such definition would not be useful to the evolution of human consciousness. The mind,

A CHINESE WOODCUT REPRESENTING THE NIRVANA OF THE BUDDHA.

HERE THE MYSTERY IS SYMBOLIZED AS THE UNIVERSALIZING OF THE PRINCIPLE OF REALIZATION THROUGH THE MEDIUM OF THE ENDLESS REPETITION OF THE BUDDHA SEATED ON A LOTUS FLOWER. IT IS OBVIOUSLY IMPOSSIBLE TO PICTURE LIBERATION. THIS IS THE WAY IN WHICH ONE ARTIST ATTEMPTED TO EXPRESS SOMETHING OF HIS CONVICTION OF THE WORLD MYSTERY

groping with an abstraction beyond its comprehension, will inevitably fall into error. It would invest Reality with the limitations and disfigurements of its own imperfect perspective. The mind would then worship these distortions as realities, and lapse into error. What the intellect cannot understand, it misunderstands. Religious misunderstandings are especially unfortunate, even tragic. They will affect every other part of the life, reducing integrity and preventing normal growth on the various planes or levels of living.

It is not wise, therefore, that the average disciple attempt in any way to anticipate ultimates. His search for Tao should result in a series of personal discoveries. Each new aspect of Tao should dawn upon him. It should come as a beautiful experience in the personal extension and impersonal awakening of the Self. There should be no preconceived opinions as to that which lies beyond. There should be open-mindedness, absolute willingness to face Truth as it is, and to rejoice in the glory of things as they are. Tao cannot be theologized. It cannot even be taught. But it can be known. The disciplines of meditation and realization are not statements of Tao *per se;* rather they are an invitation to the Taoist life. They will gradually lead toward the Real, but cannot be understood as definitions of Reality.

Earlier you have had the attempt to explain something of the mystery of the Transcendental Being; how the spirit of the personality is separated from the grosser parts to become an eighth sense. The Transcendental Being is the bridge between the objective and the subjective parts of man. Across this bridge the more refined parts of man may pass to and fro, but it is not strong enough to support the grosser aspects of the personality.

In the Nordic mythology the Transcendental Being is the Bifrost bridge, the bridge of rainbows which connects Midgard, the abode of man, with Asgard, the abode of the Heroes. Across this heroic bridge Odin of the single eye passes to and fro. The other gods and goddesses of the mundane order frequently accompany him—all except Thor, the Thunderer. Thor was of such gigantic structure and so heavy of stride that beneath his tread the bridge shook and threatened to collapse.

This charming allegory is the story of the difference between the personality and its principles. Thor of the mighty hammer, the destroyer of giants, is the human mind, the objective intellect. The mind is the conqueror of the mundane world, but it is not allowed upon the Bifrost bridge. The mind analyzes, criticizes, and divides. It is constantly given to opinions and attitudes. Its very processes shatter the subtle stuff of human aspiration. Soul power is too fragile in its early stages to bear the weight of mental criticism and intellectual analysis. Thus it is written in the Eastern classics that the mind is the slayer of the Real. As the Minotaur wandered raging in the Cretan labyrinth, so the intellect roams the world, exploring, searching, affirming and denying, building up and tearing down, conquering and being conquered, living and dying according to the laws inherent in itself. As long as there is mind there will be division. As long as there is division, intellect will contemplate and accept division. While intellect rules there is discord; but when the Self rules the intellect there is order, relationship, pattern, and purpose.

It is mind that has taught death—and according to the scriptures, death is the last great enemy. Death is a belief in limitation; a conception of existence based upon mental experience and by which the eternity of life is denied. Though all the selves may come and go, may be born and die, the Self is imperishable. There is no conflict between Reality and time. The conflict is in the mind. Reality is timeless. There is no conflict in the Self between good and evil. Evil is in the mind. Good is eternal. There is no conflict in the Self between ignorance and wisdom. Ignorance is a conception of the mind. Wisdom is eternal.

To perceive that the mind is the interposer of doubt, the very source of the impulse of negation, the root of fear, the origin of unbelief and disbelief; to discover through realization that weakness is not in the Self, but in the mind, is to emerge victorious from life's greatest battle. Armageddon is the war against the shadows that have been set up by thought.

To refer again to our Nordic myths. In the last great day the Gotterdammerung, the twilight of the gods, the heroic souls prepare themselves to do battle against the powers of darkness. And what are these powers? The armies of the shadow, the souls of the dead, wraiths riding in ships of mist, horrid apparitions loosed from the caves of Hel, monsters from under the earth, deceivers, false witnesses and false prophets, a host of vagaries riding in the ship of fools.

This is the pageantry of the lower mind; the mind which has filled the world with false doctrines and then bound man with them; the mind which has filled the air with demons and the earth with shadows; the mind which has conjured up fearsome ghouls and then prostrated itself before the productions of its own fears. The struggle between the Self and its lower selves, between realization and opinion, between illumination and thought—this is the last great war. Each must fight this battle within his own nature. Before he can proceed he must emerge victorious from his battle with his own thoughts.

It is a strange war; the strangest war of all. Man must fight without fighting. For if he opposes ignorance with any impulse of the will his realization fades away and he is left helpless. His victory must be in the simple fact of knowing, which scatters the ghosts opposing him. There is no struggle or warfare between light and darkness. When light comes, darkness fades away. Man wins by the steadfastness of his light. His victory is a gentle attainment of Truth. His enemy cannot strike back. Shadows and unrealities have no power except that which is bestowed upon them by one of the numerous attributes of ignorance. As ignorance ceases, the adversary is left powerless; but the ghosts do not return to their caverns and their grottoes. All vanish together in the presence of the knower.

The disciple must understand this without falling into further error. His realization of the unreality of the mundane order of life must not lead him into the illusion of denial. Thoughts cannot be destroyed by denying their existence, or by refusing to accept them. There is not sufficient strength or courage in any man to impel him to think down the thoughts of his world. This is why so many reformers fail. They oppose one thought with another. They try to impose an intellectual formula upon an intellectual chaos, and their formula is torn to pieces by the mind of the world that can be conquered by realization alone. In the presence of wisdom the world-mind is powerless.

Possibly this is why the world persecutes its dreamers, its mystics, its seers, its sages, and its saints. It knows that they possess a power greater than all the schemings of man. The intellect, like the fabled Herod, would protect itself by destroying the firstborn powers of the soul. The philosophy of Mahatma Gandhi (India's great religious leader), the doctrine of harmlessness, is centered about the one fundamental truth, the inevitable victory of soul power over physical power.

Again, realization must direct the course of action. The mind has its functions and its purposes. It cannot be ignored or denied, nor its significance neutralized by a gesture. Thoughts have their place in the Plan. It is realization that must put all things in their proper places. The impractical mystic, clinging to only part of the Truth, develops cults of absolutism based upon the ignoring of the mind and its phenomena. This wrong is discovered only after years of mistaken effort. We cannot deny any aspect of life. We must understand, through illusion, whatever it may be.

A concrete physical instance may help to clarify this difficult and delicate problem: Tyranny is evident in the affairs of men. Despots afflict their people; corrupt politicians exploit their states. Ambitious dictators lead their nations into ruin. To deny that such things are occurring is foolish. On the other hand, to accept the reality of tyranny, exploitation, and despotism, is equally foolish.

Where, then, is the middle ground of fact? How should a person, feeling the weight of the afflictions with which our material world is burdened, react to the conditions of his environment? The solution lies with his own inner adjustment. If his consciousness is dominated by the principle of intellect, he will accept the reality of the failure and seek to reform or oppose it. He can follow no other course for the reason that he has no other instrument of understanding with which to meet the problems. That is real to us which is similar to our own understanding. There can be no other standard of reality.

If, however, through the development of realization and the practice of the philosophic disciplines the disciple moves his inward foundation across the *antaskarana,* the bridge of consciousness, the world pattern changes because he brings a different degree of realization to that pattern. The unreality of tyranny, despotism, and exploitation is now accepted as the fact. From that time on the destructive forces of the lower world can exercise no influence upon the enlightened Self. Their significance slowly fades out. They cease, not because they have been argued down or reasoned through, but because there can be no place for them in the experience of one who has passed beyond the sphere of their influence.

A Buddhist saint once wrote: "Men drown in water and live by breathing air; fish drown in air and live by breathing the water." This is a symbolic effort to express the mystery of realization. A condition which is death to one order of life is security to another. Realization causes man to change the order of his life. The enlightened and illumined soul belongs to a race apart. He lives in a different element. Therefore, to him the laws of life are different. He transcends the world by transcending the world thought in himself. When he accomplishes this, he fulfills the admonition of the Eastern classic: "Take the sword of right and slay the slayer."

CONCLUSION

THE next few pages bring the instructions to a close. It will be your responsibility to continue the practice of the disciplines. Beginning with thoughtfulness, you must preserve a continuity of effort which will ultimately lead you beyond the world of thought and into the sphere of union with the mystical principles of life. Always bear in mind the necessity for balancing and rationalizing each step of the way so that nothing impractical or unreasonable shall deflect the consciousness from its noble purpose.

Be mystically thoughtful and thoughtfully mystical. Combine a gentle appreciation with the courage of continuous action. Permit nothing to move you from the foundations which you are building. Yet withal, retain as much as is possible of gentle human contact. Realize that wisdom brings you closer to the heart of things and sets up no artificial barriers against the free circulation of human relationships.

Do not spend too great an amount of time attempting to visualize some nirvanic state at the end of effort. Do not dream of release as freedom desired because it is the end of striving. Remember that the means and the end are one. We shall never find peace apart from the quest for peace. Beyond us lie endless vistas of progress.

The whole cosmos waits to be accomplished. Man's growing understanding and his unfolding consciousness go on in their ageless search for union with the immense principle which sustains all the mysteries of the world. It is not yet our time to contemplate finalities. The incomprehensible fascinates and intrigues, but cannot satisfy. Our greatest peace comes from the recognition of our present place in the Plan. When we know that we are trying; when we have the solid assurance that according to our various lights we are earnestly seeking, and sincerely practicing the disciplines, we enjoy what Aristotle called *well-being.*

Right-mindfulness is the direction of attention to those matters which are first in importance. Strive for a mood of mystic thoughtfulness; not merely intellectual analysis, but a kind of quickened appreciation which causes us to be attentive to the significance of living.

There was once an old Chinese scholar who enjoyed the patronage of a certain mandarin. This mandarin in a moment of generosity presented the scholar with a bullock cart. Now a bullock cart is one of the slowest methods of transportation yet devised. The ambling ox never hastens his gait, but plods along only slightly more rapidly than the average man walks. The Chinese philosopher rode in the cart the first day, but thereafter walked ahead, leading the ox. When asked why he did not make use of the conveyance the scholar replied that his newly acquired vehicle was destroying his perspective on life. Lapsing into a truly Taoist viewpoint, he explained himself thus:

"A journey, regardless of its length, is not a motion from place to place, but an experience in moving through space from place to place. In other words, man grows not as a result of arriving at his journey's end, but by the mystery of the journey itself. He learns most who travels slowly."

The sage went on to describe the adventures of his daily travel. He observed the woods at the roadside and stopped to contemplate some small natural creature fulfilling its tasks according to the impulse of instinct. Every step of his journey was alive with living purpose;

each of the objects which attracted his attention was a sermon; each embodied spiritual truth, and each bore witness to some phase of the divine Law. To hasten was to be deprived of the privilege of contact with life. It was to place the journey upon a different footing. In the comfort of his ox cart the sage could travel, but when he went on foot he experienced.

With true Oriental politeness, he compromised. He took the cart with him, but walked so that he might continue to experience his daily contact with life and at the same time might not evade the implication that he must also experience possession of the ox cart. To have rejected or returned the cart would have been, from the Taoist viewpoint, to avoid the responsibility of possession.

There is a fine point in spiritual ethics in such a dilemma. Each student would have to solve the matter in his own way. But there is no virtue in rejection, and no virtue in the performance of error to please a friend.

The most important lesson taught by the fable is that which relates to the simple journey of the day: To make the journey not because we are striving to cover a distance, but because we rejoice in a series of experiences, each of which is precious in itself. It is common in religion for the spiritual-minded to dream of the journey's end. This is a false dreaming. Rather we should be attentive to all with which we come in contact along the way. Each day of living is an experience in mystical discipline presenting new opportunities for realization; new evidence of the spiritual purpose that stands behind the worlds. The mystic is unfolding himself not because he is primarily aware of some specific goal, but because he is supremely happy in the joy of growing, and in the knowledge that he is fulfilling the destiny that was appointed to him at the beginning of all things.

To preserve a normal viewpoint in troubled times demands a high appreciation of the dignity and significance of imminent and intimate experience. We must find the Law in that which is at our hand. We must release our spiritual impulses and express our spiritual convictions here and now. It is definitely a mistake to spend too much time dreaming of lost horizons and worlds beyond. Our hopes are not fulfilled by either the dead yesterdays or the unborn tomorrows. Now and here are the time and place of fulfillment.

Theoretically it is true that somewhere and sometime consciousness will expand and finally mingle itself with the great ocean of eternity. Sometime the oneness of life will be fully realized and only the One will remain. But for us such dreaming may lead to impractical vagaries of speculation. We may be deflected from the very end we seek by our wrong estimation of universal values. Therefore, with all our studies we must be not only mystically aware of the Plan, but also practically aware that to serve the universe more adequately we must function within the limited area of our own understanding. The moment we depart from experience we depart from Reality.

Within this book are lessons which to learn will require years of thoughfulness and practice. The rules which are laid down and the intimations half-revealed in the text will require the most profound contemplation. If you follow these instructions it will be unnecessary for you to practice any other type of meditative or devotional exercises. It is my recommendation that you read the lessons again and again, approximately once in six months. You will be surprised to discover each time that there are points which you have overlooked, or which were not meaningful at the previous reading. As your own realization increases you will discover new meanings and more profound implications. You will also remind yourself of the principal dangers which unquestionably will recur as temptation as you proceed.

I cannot too strongly warn you of the dangers attendant upon unfortunate entanglements in cults or creeds. There is no reason why you should ever join anything in order to practice the mystical disciplines. They are universal. All life is living them. As well bind the creatures of the air as to bind man to some circumscribed system of thinking or living. Live from within yourself. If your actions bear witness to your convictions, you need no other code of spiritual ethics. If the best part of you rules the rest, you are well-governed.

Do not be lured by the hope that through some mystic formula you can advance more rapidly along the road to Tao. Even if it be presumed that such could be the case—which it cannot be—remember the Chinese sage who preferred to walk. It is not the leisure at the end which you are seeking; the leisure to live along the way and the mental capacity to live leisurely in a world of haste reveals the scholar. He hastens most who is most uncertain of his destination. Short cuts in philosophy do not exist. But if they did, the wise man would choose the longer road. He would choose it because of the adventures along its way; adventures in the mystic processes of becoming. Do not grudge the years and the lives which stretch out ahead. These are not merely periods of trial and tribulation. They are adventures in the mystery of the soul. When we bring to each day a realization sufficient for the day, every upset incident becomes alive with purpose and rich with meaning.

With all of your studies and all of your striving, preserve the inner calm which is the symbol of true spiritual development. This inward calm is not a negative impotence, nor a suspension of tension. It is true peace, strong, gentle, and filled with understanding. It is a sort of axis about which rotates the ever-turning wheel of your objective existence. Your own inner peace is the motionless center of the moving world.

As one of the great classics of the East says: "The universe turns upon the axis of silence." This must be true in your own life. The calm serenity which circles all the phenomena of your living is your nirvana. It bears witness to the realization that you have actually achieved. It is the symbol of your real strength; the strength of silence; the power of quietude. Once having attained this inward poise, never depart from it. Cause it to increase. Transmute into it, little by little, all the elements of outer living.

Beware of early enthusiasm! It easily fails. So many persons start enterprises enthusiastically and far too energetically. In a short time they discover that they cannot maintain the high key of their initial impulse. They begin well and end badly.

Do not begin the practice of the disciplines with some grand, intensive resolution. To do so is to become weary after a little time. Begin gently, satisfied to proceed at a rate of speed comparable with understanding and the restrictions imposed by environment.

Be sure that your growth is not accomplished at the expense of responsibilities, and be not overhasty to convert others to your ideas. Let the obvious improvement in your own nature convert them.

Do not become discouraged once you begin the disciplines. They must become as much a part of your life as eating or sleeping. They belong to you. They must be practiced from now on throughout time, not merely as a ritual but as a quality of yourself, with the same acceptance of them as is expressed by the natural processes of eating and digesting of food. After a time you will no longer realize that you are practicing a discipline. It will be part of your life. You will instinctively include realization in all the modes and moods of your existence It will be as natural to realize as to think; as normal to understand as to feel. Awareness and thoughtfulness will become part of you, and altogether your inward education will result in a great responsiveness to life—which is the basis of true greatness.

Under such conditions it will be impossible for you to determine with certainty where realization mingles with illumination, for each is a part of the other. You never will know the time when you transcend thought and rise into the mindless vistas of true spiritual apperception. Yet as you proceed, all of the transcendental processes which you are building up will manifest themselves, until from their blending and mingling will come the true enlightenment of the initiated sage.

Most sublime of all is the mystic truth that long before illumination crowns your effort you will have forgotten illumination. You will be so absorbed in the experiencing of God, that like the Sufi in his rapture you will forget to be mindful of yourself. The time will never come when you will rapturously exclaim, "I am illuminated." You will never stand aside to marvel at your own superiority.

You will never ponder thoughtfully as to whether you are ready for nirvana, nor will you ever ask yourself what lies beyond the world. As realization brings these great extensions of consciousness to you, you will be so perfectly conditioned to receive them that you will neither wonder nor be surprised. You will be neither glad nor sorry in the terms of human emotion. You will experience merely an extension of the law of cause and effect. Illumination will come because it is necessary. You will need it in order that you may continue to experience your participation in Reality.

The mystical disciplines are the natural, human way to Truth. They are available to all men, and each who attempts the living of them is rewarded according to his integrity and his continuity. As time finally mingles in the ocean of eternity, so all creatures who live in time finally will mingle with the one nature that abides in eternity. Our journey is from here to the forever along gentle roads of growth. It is our own lack of understanding that has made these roads difficult and has obstructed nature with a thousand artificial hazards and predicaments. But as long as men remain, as long as humanity endures, the search for Truth will be the same search, the means will be the same, and the end will be the same. The disciples of all ages shall assume the contemplative life, and through the harmless practice of realization seek *Union*.

TWELFTH REALIZATION

As the closing realization, remember that we must be thoughtful through the years—not during the practice of a series of lessons, or even through a series of lives. Realization must go on until it achieves identity with the object of itself.

Let your realization through all this time be that simply, naturally, gently, normally, and happily, you are growing up through the many to the One, and that you are accomplishing this through the gradual processes of discovering as a series of joyous experiences the One in each of the many. Realization is the conscious understanding of the unity of life, and of the unity of the living Self with the deathless Cause which abides in the innermost parts of the world.

Be patient, and in all things be kind—and time and eternity will be patient and kind through you.